MANASSAS
to
APPOMATTOX

The Civil War Memoirs of
Pvt. Edgar Warfield
17th Virginia Infantry

EPM PUBLICATIONS, INC.
McLean, Virginia

Library of Congress Cataloging-in-Publication Data

Warfield, Edgar, 1842-1934.
    [Confederate soldier's memoirs]
    Manassas to Appomattox : the war memoirs of Edgar Warfield,
    17th Virginia Infantry, C.S.A.
        p.   cm.
    Includes index.
    Originally published: A Confederate soldier's memoirs. Richmond :
    Masonic Home Press, Inc., 1936.
        ISBN 1-889324-04-3
    1. Warfield, Edgar, 1842-1934. 2. Confederate States of America.
Army. Virginia Infantry Regiment, 17th. 3. Soldiers—Virginia—
Alexandria—Biography. 4. Virginia—History—Civil War, 1861-1865—
Personal narratives. 5. United States—History—CivilWar,
1861-1865—Personal narratives, Confederate. 6. Alexandria (Va.)—
Biography. I. Title.
E581.5 17th.W37   1996
973.7'455—dc21   96-48089
                                                                             CIP

EPM Publications, Inc., 1003 Turkey Run Road,
    McLean, VA 22101
Printed in the United States of America

Cover design by Tom Huestis

Cover & title page photograph:
    Edgar Warfield, at the beginning of the Civil War. Age 18, 1861.
    Courtesy, a Friend of Fort Ward

PREFACE

Originally published in 1936 under the title "A Confederate Soldier's Memoirs," Private Edgar Warfield provides a wealth of detailed information on daily life in the Confederate army. His well-written narrative of his wartime experiences in Company H, 17th Virginia Infantry stands on its own merits and is reissued by the Friends of Fort Ward without change.

The Friends of Fort Ward are indebted to EPM Publications for recognizing the historical value of Warfield's story. We would like to recognize William Smith, The Lyceum, and a Friend of Fort Ward for the photographs that are included in the book. The Friends are also indebted to the Alexandria Library, Lloyd House for research assistance with the index, and to the staff of Fort Ward Museum for their supervision and editorial assistance in bringing this project to completion.

The Friends of Fort Ward
Alexandria, Virginia

INTRODUCTORY

PRIMARILY this book is being published as a token of love and respect for our father, the late Edgar Warfield, who died November 26, 1934. During all his long life of ninety-two years he was a resident of Alexandria, and he was known and held in affectionate regard by an exceptionally large circle of friends. It is particularly with these friends in mind that we are printing his reminiscences of four years' arduous service in the War Between the States. We hope they will find in the book much that is interesting in itself, but also that their interest may be greatly intensified because they were so intimately acquainted with its author.

A second reason for printing the book, however, will appeal to the public at large. Seventy years have now passed since the close of the great conflict between the American states. Very, very few are now living who had a part in the tremendous drama. Soon no one will be left who can describe its scenes from first-hand experience. It is important, therefore, that all records of such first-hand impressions shall be carefully gathered up and preserved, to form an ever more valuable record of how the war appeared to those who actually carried it on. This is especially true of the experiences of the private soldier, which all too often have escaped recording in the general interest in the larger aspects of the conflict.

Edgar Warfield served the full four years of the war as a private in the Seventeenth Virginia Infantry. His experience covered the complete span of the fighting in Virginia, as he was present at the defense of Blackburn's Ford, the opening skirmish of the First Battle of Manassas and he was a member of the last Confederate outpost at Appomattox when Lee returned from the surrender of his army to Grant. In between he shared to the full in the hard fighting, the strenuous marches, and on too many occasions the extreme privations of the warfare in the Virginia sector. He was a member of Robert E. Lee's Army of Northern Virginia, an army that ranks as one of the finest of all history in fighting spirit and discipline. He had a part in all its major engagements except Chancellorsville, Gettysburg, and the Wilderness, and his regiment, the Seventeenth Virginia, was one of the famous units of that army, being singled out for special praise by General Lee and by the Legislature of Virginia.

At the outbreak of the war he was a youth of eighteen, having been born June 7, 1842. He was the second of nine children. His father was Abel Davis Warfield, described as a man of large stature and whole-souled, jovial disposition whom everyone liked. His mother before her marriage was Sarah Ann Adams, and judging from the one or two glimpses we have of her in the present narrative was a woman of intrepid courage and spirit. Both parents were natives of Maryland and the father was a member of the well-known Warfield family of that state. They were married in Washington July 1, 1838, and their first two children, George and Edgar, were born in that city. The family presently removed to Alexandria and its name has continued to identified with that city ever since.

At the beginning of 1861 Edgar Warfield was a clerk in the drug store of Wat Tyler Cluverius. After the war he returned to the drug business and remained in it during all his active business life. When he retired he found time to cultivate more actively his various side interests, among which were especially Confederate veteran activities and all that pertained to the war. Some years after the war's close he had begun to write down now and then some of the features of his experiences which he remembered best but the notes were scattered and incomplete. In his later years he took them up again and completed them. It was his habit to retire to his room after dinner in the evening and spend a few hours before bedtime in writing up his recollections and living again through the scenes which they brought to mind. Although he was around ninety years of age when he wrote them out the handwriting is as clear, firm, and legible as that of a man of twenty-five or thirty, and the stories are quite evidently the outgivings of a memory still undimmed.

In preparing the notes for publication only such slight changes have been made in them as were necessary to a more perfect arrangement of the narrative. This editorial work has been done by Mr. Otto Wilson, of Washington, D. C.

EDGAR WARFIELD, JR.,
GEORGE E. WARFIELD.

Alexandria, Va., November 1, 1935.

CONTENTS

A CONFEDERATE SOLDIER'S MEMOIRS

CHAPTER I

FOREWORD

"WHY does not someone give an account of the occurrences in our city just prior to its evacuation by our soldiers in 1861?"

That question I have heard many times. It furnishes the real reason why I began the writing of these private reminiscences, although they later broadened out to cover the whole period of the war. I felt that I had data with which to satisfy to some extent the desire of those who wished to know more of the history of our good old town at the time when the war clouds were gathering. And I felt, too, that the reading of the lines might also recall to the minds of some who lived in those days incidents familiar to them.

I became a member of the Old Dominion Rifles (afterwards Company H, Seventeenth Virginia Infantry) at its organization, December 6, 1860. From the date of its organization until the close of the war I continued a member of that company. During the entire four years I was absent from my command only fourteen days, while I was on furlough, and I rejoined it in the trenches at Bermuda Hundred on the James River, between Richmond and Petersburg, while it was still holding the same position on the line as when I left. This was the only leave I had during my entire enlistment. Also during the entire war, with the exception of two weeks when I was sick, I never slept once under a roof.

My company, the Old Dominion Rifles, had the proud distinction of never having had a conscript or drafted man added to its ranks during the entire war. This was because the number of men on its rolls never fell below the minimum of twenty-eight.

The accounts here given of conditions in our city in 1860 and 1861 and of such incidents as came under my observation during the war are taken chiefly from my personal recollections. There seems to be no complete record to which one can refer. The volumes of the Alexandria Gazette for those years are missing from the files kept by the city, but are complete up to and including 1859. However, I do have one valuable aid to my memory. A few years after the war, at the solicitation of my family, I jotted down many personal reminiscences simply as a family paper, with no thought that any part of them would ever be published. These notes were laid aside for a number of years and then were taken up again and completed.

These notes were written chiefly in the hope that in future years the reading of them might give pleasure to members of the family, as a reminder of the many pleasant hours we spent together at the home fireside while I told of my recollections of camp life and march while a private in the Army of the Potomac and the Army of Northern Virginia. But I also look upon them as the product of a duty performed. For I believe it to be the duty of every Confederate soldier to record his own experiences during these eventful four years, whether he writes of the heroism of the battlefield or the humors of the camp and bivouac.

These matters should be put on record by the still living actors in those scenes, now so rapidly decreasing in number, in order that their children and their children's children may know what manner of men their forefathers were - that they may know them as men who, sacrificing all the comforts of home, leaving their dear ones, and abandoning a state of peace and security, offered their lives in so unequal a contest with a unanimity almost unparalleled; rallied to the defense of the land they loved; took up arms in defense of principles dearer to them than life; and defended those principles with a courage and valor unsurpassed.

In the accounts that follow I am aware that I may have repeated some things that have been told by others. But my whole desire has been simply to tell of some incidents that came under my own observation and to put them in their proper setting. If they seem rambling and disconnected, it must be remembered that they have been jotted down from time to time merely to put in written form the stories I have so often told at the fireside, or in the company of old comrades as we fought our battles over again. It must be remembered too that these are the experiences of a private soldier. I have had little to tell of the great conflicts in which mighty armies were engaged. These matters I leave to the recognized historians, many of whom have carefully gathered facts and figures and given to the world the meritorious result of their labors - though there are others, I must add, who have so distorted the facts that we who were actually participants in the scenes described can hardly recognize them.

Finally, it has not been my intention to write of the long, weary march with all its attendant suffering, its dust, heat, and thirst, or to relate the horrors of the battlefield on which so many of our loved ones offered up their lives a sacrifice to the cause that failed, except as these things are recalled sadly by the thoughts of our dead comrades. Rather I have tried to tell of the cheerful, joyous scenes of camp life and the march, of the many hours spent by the burning log, of the stories told, the many jests, and above all the happy, rollicking songs by Hurdle, Smith, Kidwell, Roxbury, and others of the Old Dominion Rifles that would rise in the still night air and make the very woods ring with melody.

These moments around the blazing camp-fire, after all, were the happiest of the soldier's life in the field. For it was then, while gazing into the blaze and glow of the coals, that he would give himself up to thoughts of home and the loved ones there. Around the fire the closest friendships were formed while we talked together, and while our hearts went out in sympathy to the comrade who was then on the lonely vigil of sentinel and picket.

CHAPTER II

THE WAR CLOUDS GATHER

TO see the beginnings of the war properly we have to go back to the days of 1859-61. Those were the days when all was bright and joyous in our dear old town. Gayly clad volunteers marched gallantly through the streets, with bands playing and drums rolling, amid the waving of flags by fair hands. New and dazzling uniforms helped to make a bright and cheerful picture for the eyes of the young soldier. All too soon the picture was to be changed by the stern realities of war. The grime, sweat, dust, and blood of the conflict were to make those bright uniforms sadly war-worn, and hunger was to get in its dreadful work, making haggard and emaciated the once bright and happy faces.

It was following the John Brown insurrection at Harper's Ferry, which took place on Sunday night, October 16, 1859, that the war clouds began to gather and trouble was in sight. From that time the people of the South, anticipating trouble, began organizing military companies throughout the various sections. At that time the military force of our city consisted of the Alexandria Riflemen, Captain Morton Marye; the Mount Vernon Guards, Captain Samuel H. Devaughn; and the Alexandria Artillery, Captain George Duffey. These three companies took an active part in the suppression of the raid.

At the time of the John Brown insurrection Colonel Robert E. Lee, of the Second Regiment, United States Cavalry, was at Arlington, his home, awaiting orders. On Monday, the 17th, he received the following order from the War Department:

> "War Department,
> Adjutant General's Office,
> Washington, October 17, 1859.

"Special Orders
    No. 194
    "Brevet Colonel R. E. Lee, Second Cavalry, is assigned to duty according to his brevet rank, and will command the troops ordered to

Harper's Ferry Armory, under the instructions given him personally by the Secretary of War.

"By order of the Secretary of War.
"E.D. Townsend,
Assistant Adjutant General."

The instructions were to take command of a battalion of marines, proceed to Harper's Ferry, and "take such measures as in his judgment may be necessary to protect the Arsenal and other property of the United States" at that place.

The mounted messenger who had been sent to Colonel Lee learned at Arlington that he had gone to Alexandria on business, and received the addresses of several business houses in that city at which he might be found. The soldier continued on to Alexandria and found the colonel at Leadbeater's Drug Store, in conversation with the proprietor, Mr. Edward S. Leadbeater, Sr., and there delivered his message.

After reading the order the colonel remarked to Mr. Leadbeater, with whom he was intimately acquainted:

"Ned, I am afraid that this is the beginning of much more serious trouble."

The colonel immediately left and reported at Washington, took command of the battalion of marines, and proceeded to Harper's Ferry by train, reaching that place at 11 o'clock p. m. There he found a force of Virginia militia that had hastily gathered to the place, including the Alexandria Riflemen. The company had left Alexandria on Sunday night under orders from the governor of Virginia, Henry A. Wise.

The bearer of the message who had been sent to Arlington for Colonel Lee was no other than Lieutenant J. E. B. Stuart, of the First U.S. Cavalry, who afterwards became the great cavalry leader of the Army of Northern Virginia. At that time he was at the War Department on business and volunteered to carry the message. Immediately on his return to the Department he asked and obtained permission to accompany Colonel Lee to Harper's Ferry as his aid, and he was the officer sent by Colonel Lee under a flag of truce to demand the surrender of Brown. Brown refused, and on Tuesday morning, at sunrise,

11

Lieutenant Green of the marines, with twelve men, broke in the door of the engine house in which the insurgents had barricaded themselves and captured the entire party, also releasing a number of citizens whom Brown was holding as hostages. This brought the insurrection to an end.

Our Alexandria troops returned, but because of rumors that organized bands were coming from the north to attempt a rescue of Brown our three Alexandria companies were ordered to Charlestown to guard the prisoners and attend the trial and, later, the execution of Brown and his followers. The trial resulted in a verdict of guilty, and the prisoners were hung, December 2, 1859. An extract from a Washington paper stated that at the time of the execution at Charlestown a bell in the steeple of the church located at the northeast corner of sixth and D Streets was tolled in mournful sympathy, but this was not with the approval of the authorities.

Colonel Lee, in his report to the Adjutant General, dated October 19, made mention of the Virginia volunteers as follows:

"The promptness with which the volunteer troops repaired to the scene of disturbance and the alacrity they displayed to suppress the gross outrage against law and order, I know will elicit your hearty approbation."

Shortly after the close of the John Brown disorders Lieutenant Colonel Lee was again on his way to Texas to assume his official duties. There he remained until he was summoned to Washington in February, 1861. He arrived on March 1 and on the 16th following was appointed Colonel of the First U. S. Cavalry.

While the three Alexandria companies were on duty at Charlestown it was deemed necessary to form a Home Guard for service in the city. This was done in November, 1859, the following officers being elected: Captain, W. S. Kemper; First Lieutenant, M. D. Corse; Second Lieutenant, Charles F. Suttle; Third Lieutenant, R. A. Ashby; Fourth Lieutenant, Thornton Triplett.

This corps was composed of citizens without regard to age or liability to military service. Many were included who had long passed the time when they could legally be called upon for such service. Concerning it the Washington Star (as quoted in the Alexandria

12

Gazette, November 30, 1859) said:

"By way of illustrating the intensity of the feeling throughout Virginia, with reference to the shape the 'irrepressible conflict' has assumed through the practical working of John Brown and his band, we may mention that the new Alexandria company, styled the 'Home Guard', numbered more than a hundred men, more than one-half of whom were over fifty years of age, and that there were not a few persons carrying muskets in its ranks worth from one hundred thousand to nearly half a million dollars."

CHAPTER III

MILITARY COMPANIES IN ALEXANDRIA

ON December 1, 1860, a notice appeared in the Alexandria Gazette signed by two boys, Frank Wise and Edgar Warfield, calling on all boys between sixteen and twenty years of age who wished to unite in forming a rifle company to meet at the banking house of the Corse Brothers, which was located in the Exchange Building, 417-19 King Street.

Only four persons responded to this call, and one of these was just a visitor. The third recruit was Seabury D. Smith. Undiscouraged, the three boys continued the work of recruiting members, and on December 6, 1860, at American Hall, the armory of the Alexandria Riflemen on Cameron Street, a total of sixty-eight members answered roll call and the company was immediately organized. It selected as its name "The Old Dominion Rifles" and adopted a uniform, and on the night of January 7, 1861, completed its organization by electing the following officers: Captain, Montgomery D. Corse; First Lieutenant, Arthur Herbert; Second Lieutenant, William H. Fowle, Jr.; Third Lieutenant, Douglass F. Forrest.

The non-commissioned officers were: First Sergeant, W. W. Zimmerman; Second Sergeant, George Siggers; Third Sergeant, Thomas S. Smoot; Fourth Sergeant, S. R. Shinn; First Corporal, Albion Hurdle; Second Corporal, James E. Green; Third Corporal, James H. Fowle; Fourth Corporal, James F. Grimes; Surgeon, Dr. Harold Snowden; Secretary, Thomas S. Fitzhugh; Treasurer, Frank Wise.

The uniform adopted at this meeting was to be of "Virginia made cadet gray cloth, a jacket of the pattern of the Hungarian Riflemen, the Zouave pants, the cap after the style of the French infantry, all trimmed with green, and the Virginia State buttons, and with short boots." In order to expedite the uniforming of the company we were ordered to have our measures taken for uniforms immediately. The contract for them was given to Mr. George Harper, a merchant tailor of the city, and our officers guaranteed the entire amount, simply taking our individual notes. Each uniform cost $22.00.

In those days all military companies were required to furnish their own uniforms, as well as to provide armories in which to meet and drill. In fact, all expenses were borne by the companies, the state furnishing only guns and equipment.

Shortly after the formation of the company a major inspector arrived from Richmond to muster it into the state service. The men were formed in line, and the major began his inspection. On his rounds he drew from the ranks some five or six boys, of whom I was one.

I walked over to the Captain and asked what it meant, and he in turn asked the major, who replied that I was too small for service. I immediately protested, telling him that I was one of the organizers of the company and ought on that account to receive some consideration. I also told him that so far as size was concerned I was as tall as the captain, who was short and rather stout. The major, some what amused, told me to "back up" against Captain Corse. I did so, and the test proved that I was a fraction of an inch taller than my captain. And so, with Captain Corse vouching for my fitness to be a soldier, I was mustered into the service of the State of Virginia. The others who were rejected by this officer eventually returned and became members.

This company, from first to last, carried on its rolls 111 members. On the day of its departure from the city it numbered over 100. Only one of that number was over twenty-one years of age, and only one was married, his marriage occurring just prior to our leaving. And he did not see his wife again until the war closed.

The officers of the Old Dominion Rifles, all of whom were soon by their gallant deportment to shed luster on the arms of the service they had entered, immediately set to work to bring the company up to the highest standard of military excellence. They employed as a drill master one Captain Charles A. Bragonier, who was certainly as fine an instructor in military tactics as one would wish. Under his teaching the company became one of the best drilled organizations of its day.

We had indeed plenty of competition, for many other companies were also drilling. Alexandria could well boast of the smartness of its soldiers in 1861. The usual spirit of rivalry always to be found when two or more such organizations exist side by side began to show itself among our volunteers. But with our gay and jaunty uniforms of Hungarian jackets and Zouave pants and with the youthfulness of our membership we carried, or thought we did, the smiles of the fair ones with us.

This was manifest most in the afternoons, when we held our company drills on the old Catalpa lot, located just beyond and opposite to the Mount Vernon cotton factory on North Washington Street. There we were required to drill for an hour each afternoon and there the ladies of the city, both young and old, congregated to witness our evolutions. The Old Dominion Rifles at that time had the advantage of all the others in the attractiveness of their drill. We were considered nearly perfect in the skirmish drill, the movements of which were carried out to the sounds of a bugle.

Of the other Alexandria companies formed or being formed in those days, the older ones have been mentioned. The Alexandria Riflemen were organized in 1856. An amusing story is told in connection with the name of this fine company. The organization meeting was held in the old Exchange Building, on the north side of King Street between Royal and Pitt Streets. The name "Alexandria Sharp Shooters" was determined upon and a uniform selected, and it was decided that the knapsacks and cartridge boxes should be covered with a flap of highly polished patent leather, on which were to be stamped in gilt letters the initials of the company and the year of its organization.

After the meeting had adjourned some of the members lingered in the street before the hall, engaged in conversation. It occurred to someone to figure out how the initials of the company would look on the knapsacks. But when he had done so and called his comrades' attention to them there was a pause of consternation. For the initials of the company were A. S. S.! Obviously that would never do. Some of the members might be possessed of asinine qualities, but there was no reason for advertising the fact so conspicuously. Moreover, what would be the delight of the small urchins of the town when they found that the smart new military company was publicly announcing its members to be donkeys! And how could they ever face the young ladies? There was but one thing to do. Captain Marye hastily shouted for the members to reassemble, a quorum was obtained, and the name was unanimously changed to "Alexandria Riflemen". Under this name the company was mustered into the service of the State of Virginia, and into that of the Confederate States at the outbreak of the war, and under it the company fought gallantly throughout the four years of the struggle.

On December 2, 1860, a cavalry company was formed. On December 13 a meeting was held at the Relief Engine House for the purpose of organizing a new rifle company, but it failed to materialize. Later another effort was made at the Friendship Engine House to form a company. Sixty-five men were enrolled, officers were elected, and the name "The Letcher Guards" adopted, in honor of the governor of the state. This venture, too, for some unknown reason proved a failure, though many of those interested in it enrolled with the other companies before they left the city.

One of the older companies of the city was the Alexandria Artillery. On the night of January 10, 1861, at Phoenix Hall, on the third story of the building on the northwest corner of King and Royal Streets, it elected Delaware Kemper as its Captain, succeeding Captain George Duffey. Captain Duffey had received his commission on July 29, 1850, from Lieutenant Governor R. T. Daniel. On July 8, 1858, he had been promoted to the rank of Major, and on January 2, 1861, he was raised to the rank of lieutenant colonel of artillery of Virginia. The company up to this time had been assigned to the Second Regiment, Second Division, Virginia Militia.

On February 19, 1861, four companies were brought together to form the Alexandria Battalion. These four companies were the Old Dominion Rifles, the Alexandria Riflemen, the Mount Vernon Guards, and the Alexandria Artillery. Captain Corse, of our company, was elected major, thus advancing all the company's commissioned officers. First Sergeant W. W. Zimmerman was made third lieutenant.

About this time two other companies were formed, composed mainly of our Irish fellow citizens. These were the Emmett Guards, with James E. Towson as captain, W. H. Kemper as first lieutenant, Robert F. Knox as second lieutenant, and Charles W. Wattles as third lieutenant; and the O'Connell Guards, the officers of which were: Captain, S. W. Prestman; first lieutenant, Raymond Fairfax; second lieutenants, H. S. Wallace and James E. Green.

Even the boys of our city caught the military fever and

17

organized a company whose members were between the ages of twelve and fifteen. They uniformed themselves, called themselves the "Young Riflemen", and drilled with wooden guns. They were about fifty in number. Colonel Charles E. Stuart, commanding the 175th Regiment, Virginia Militia, promised them regular equipment from the state when they enrolled the requisite number of sixty. They used as an armory the second floor of the building on the southwest corner of King and Columbus Streets. The boys offered their services to the governor but because of their youth the offer was declined. Several of the older boys received carbines, however, and a number of them enlisted in the other companies and went south with them.*

The 175th Regiment, Virginia Militia, held an annual drill on the Catalpa lot on North Washington Street. It was commanded at this time by Colonel Charles E. Stuart, Lieutenant Colonel H. Carter Dorsey, and Major William T. Padgett. The organization ceased to exist when the enrollment for the impending war began.

Besides the various companies of home troops, the city's garrison came to include, in February, 1861, several volunteer companies from outside in nearby Virginia. These were the Warrenton Rifles, Captain John Q. Marr; the Prince William Rifles, Captain J. S. Hamilton; the Fairfax Rifles, Captain William H. Dulaney; and the Loudoun Guards, Captain C. B. Tebbs. The Loudoun Cavalry, Captain Shreeves, was here for a few days, occupying quarters at the northwest corner of Fairfax and Queen Streets (Coyle's stables).

At about this time a number of men from Washington who had determined to cast their lot with the South came to our city and organized, in Phoenix Hall, four companies of infantry. One of these was under a Captain Reuben Cleary, another under Captain Cornelius Boyle, and another under a Captain Sherman. These were styled the Washington Volunteers. The fourth company, under Captain Frank B. Schaeffer, was known as the Beauregard Rifles and was made up of former members of the National Rifles of Washington.

In connection with this fourth company, General Charles P.

---

*A partial roll of this company of boys is given in the Appendix.

18

Stone, of the U. S. Army, after the war wrote a long article for the *Century Magazine* entitled "Washington on the Eve of War". As the war approached, he said, there were only four volunteer military companies in Washington. He was directed to reorganize them and ascertain their loyalty, as the authorities were doubtful whether they could be relied upon or not in case of trouble. He soon became convinced that three of them could be depended upon to be loyal, but the fourth, the National Rifles, showed several suspicious features. It was remarkable for its accurate drill and full ranks, it was recruiting its membership in a lively manner, and it had more than its allotment of arms and ammunition. When these facts were disclosed Captain Schaeffer, finding he was suspected, resigned and brought with him to Alexandria all the other members who were in sympathy with the South. General Stone believed that he broke up a plan to seize the public departments at the proper moment and obtain possession of the seals of government. Captain Schaeffer's part was said to be to form a battalion and take possession of the Treasury Department for the benefit of the new provisional government.

When regiments were organized at Manassas the Washington Volunteers became a part of the Seventh Virginia Regiment of Infantry. The Beauregard Rifles participated in the Battle of Manassas unassigned. After that fight it was commanded by Lieutenant Cummings. These companies had not received their guns up to the time of leaving Alexandria.

CHAPTER IV

BETWEEN PEACE AND WAR

DURING these early months of 1861 we could almost see the skies grow steadily darker. War became practically a certainty. In Alexandria the training of the volunteers went steadily forward, and one event after another gave evidence of how the public was changing over from a civilian to a military status.

The annual celebration of the anniversary of the birth of George Washington took place as usual on February 22, but there was a significance to the event which had not been known before. In the parade marched the Loudoun Guards of Leesburg and the Warren Rifles of Front Royal, in addition to our own companies and to the Fire Department organizations, consisting of the Sun, Hydraulion, Friendship, Star, and Relief companies. The military company of boys, the "Young Riflemen," were also a proud feature of the parade. On the same day, in front of Lyceum Hall, a handsome Virginia State flag was presented to the Alexandria Riflemen by the ladies of the city, the presentation speech being made by Mr. Francis L. Smith, Sr., and the speech of acceptance by the company's Captain, Morton Marye.

On March 10 the Alexandria Artillery had its first inspection. On the 19th Colonel Charles F. Suttle was elected captain of the Home Guards, succeeding Captain W. S. Kemper, who had resigned on account of feeble health. On the 28th the Old Dominion Rifles took the field for their first practice of the skirmish drill. On April 1 a concert was given for the benefit of the Old Dominion Rifles at Liberty Hall on Cameron Street, the company attending in uniform.

On March 15 Lincoln issued his proclamation calling for 75,000 troops to quell the rebellion in the South. In pursuance of this call a letter was sent by the Secretary of War to the governors of the different states, that to Governor Letcher, of Virginia, calling for three regiments, approximately 3,000 men, for that purpose. The Governor made prompt reply, as follows:

"In reply to this communication I have only to say that the militia of Virginia *will not be furnished* to the powers at Washington for any such use or purpose as they have in view. Your object is to subjugate the Southern States, and a requisition made upon me for such an object, an object in my judgment not within the purview of the Constitution or the Act of 1795, *will not be complied with.* You have chosen to inaugurate civil war, and, having done so, we will meet it in a spirit as determined as the administration has exhibited toward the South."

Two days later, on the 17th, the Virginia Convention passed the Ordinance of Secession, which was to be voted upon for ratification on Thursday, May 23. The Convention had unanimously adopted the following resolution:

"The people of Virginia recognize the American principle that government is founded on the consent of the governed. They assert the right of the people of the several states of this Union for just cause to withdraw from their association, under the Federal Government, with the people of the other states, and to erect new governments. And they never will consent that the Federal power, which is in part their power, shall be exerted for the purpose of subjecting such states to the Federal authority."

The adoption by the convention of this ordinance was followed on the 20th by the resignation of Colonel Robert E. Lee from the First Cavalry Regiment, U. S. Army. He was immediately called to Richmond and on April 22 was offered the command of the military and naval forces of the state.

On the 20th of this month Captain E. B. Powell organized a company of cavalry, which left this city with the other companies on the morning of our evacuation. This company was composed mainly of recruits from the adjoining county of Fairfax. It was known during the war as the Fairfax Cavalry.

On April 21 the following order was sent by the War Department at Washington to the commanding officer at Fort Washington, on the Potomac River just below our city:

"Sir: The steamer *Monticello,* from New York, is expected soon to arrive in the river, perhaps some time today, having supplies for this place (Washington), which will undoubtedly be seized if the boat is allowed to go to Alexandria. The General in Chief directs that you bring her to, and keep her under the protection of the guns of your fort, until a safe convoy can be provided.

"E. D. Townsend,

Assistant Adjutant General."

In connection with this order I recall that while on duty at the foot of Cameron Street I noticed a long-boat loading provisions destined for Fort Washington. They had been purchased from our local merchants. When the boat was ready to leave I told the captain that he could not depart without a permit from our military authorities. He started an argument, but I called for the sergeant of the guard, who put an extra guard on the boat and it was not allowed to leave.

During this time our battalion regularly performed guard duty, and continued to do so until the evacuation of the city, which occurred early on the morning of Friday, May 24, 1861.

The troops here were quartered in different sections of the city. The Alexandria Riflemen were at the northeast corner of King and Columbus Streets. The Mount Vernon Guards were on the west side of Fairfax Street, between King and Prince Streets, in the present Harlow Building and the one adjoining.

The first quarters of the Old Dominion Rifles were at 515 King Street but they were later removed to Peyton's Grove, near the upper end of King Street. The Emmett and O'Connell guards were stationed at 210 Prince Street, between Fairfax and Lee. The Warren Rifles of Front Royal had quarters on the north side of Cameron Street, between Fairfax and Royal (at the point where the Belvoir Hotel now stands), and Ball's Cavalry on Duke Street, near the old Orange and Alexandria station, in what is now the Norman Apartments. The other companies were quartered in different parts of the city. The Alexandria Artillery at this time was at Manassas, where it had been sent several days before.

During our service in this city permission was frequently granted for the men to sleep at their homes at night. In case of an emergency call the town bell would be rung, sounding the military call and summoning the men to their armories. To my recollection this alarm was given only once. I was caught at home. The alarm was caused by a report that the enemy was crossing into Virginia at the Chain Bridge, above Georgetown. The report proved to be false, but we were not allowed to return to our homes, being kept under arms until daylight.

Guard duty at that time was rather pleasant. Certain posts were very desirable, especially those near which some of our popular young ladies lived. The post most sought by the boys was that on the south side of King Street between Henry and Fayette, and many were the tricks and maneuvers resorted to in order to get posted on that and other desirable stations.

On this particular post eatables and drinkables were plentiful at all times, and until a late hour there was also the company of bright and pretty girls. As an added attraction a Mr. Martin, who owned a brewery at the corner of Fayette and Commerce Streets (No. 802) and who lived just opposite at the southeast corner of King and Fayette Streets, kept a keg of ale on tap in his front vestibule for the benefit of those who cared to indulge.

Many are the stories told by the boys in the service at that time of adventures they met with while on guard duty around the city.

I call to mind one little incident that occurred while I was standing guard on North Washington Street. My post extended from the corner of Princess Street (where the rectory of Christ Church now stands) to the north end of the cotton-factory block, where I was met by the other sentry, whose post extended from that point to beyond the old canal basin.

This post was held by Billie Wright, of the Alexandria Riflemen, a comrade somewhat older than myself. While we were talking a fight occurred in one of a row of houses (still in existence) across the commons, between an Irishman and his wife. At that time there were a great many Irish in the city, drawn by the coal trade, which was very large and employed many hands.

The fight continued so long that Billie thought it was our duty to go across the square and try to put an end to it. I argued that we should not leave our posts for such a purpose but Billie, who was a lively sort of fellow and always ready for fun and frolic, thought this was a golden opportunity for a little excitement. I finally yielded and went with him. In the meantime the fight had grown warmer and a number of others, both men and women, were taking sides, some with the old man and others with the old woman. It began to look like a free-for-all.

I tried again to persuade my comrade not to interfere, but no, nothing would do but he must go in. Well, he went. In the twinkling of an eye the participants on both sides quit fighting each other, and making common cause turned on him. With a clean pitch on their part, out came Billie, gun and all, on to the sidewalk, nearly upsetting me in his hasty exit. It took but very little more argument on my part to convince him that we had no business there; and so the military beat a hasty retreat.

On May 1, 1861, our Virginia forces were called out. Two days later the governor of the state called for additional troops. Between the time when we commenced guard duty and the date of our final departure from Alexandria my company was twice ordered from the city. The first time we were sent to Culpeper Court House, but only for a day or two. During the last week in April we were ordered to Warrenton, where we spent two very pleasant weeks. While there our company was called upon to take the oath of allegiance to the state, which was done unanimously.

On our return from Warrenton we found the gunboat *Pawnee* lying anchored in the middle of the channel, just opposite Cameron Street, with her guns run out, commanding the city. She had arrived from Washington on May 12.

While on duty there one night, listening to the cry of the sentinel "All's Well!" from the deck of the *Pawnee*, I challenged in the darkness a figure coming down the street. It proved to be a former schoolmate of mine, A. P. Eastlack, whose family, on account of the father's strong Union feeling and offensive manner of proclaiming it, had been ordered to leave the city on the following day.

My companion had come to bid me goodbye. Unknown to his parents he had risen from his bed and stolen out on his errand at midnight. He was of about my age and had been my closest friend at school. Had he been allowed to follow his own inclination he would have enlisted with me and followed the fortunes of the Confederacy. The poor fellow left in tears, and I did not see him again until after the war.

One night during the period of our occupation of Alexandria, while I was engaged with Sergeant George Wise at the barracks making cartridges for our rifles, we were taken from our work about twelve

24

o'clock by Lieutenant Fowle for a scout up the Washington road. Our scout extended beyond the Columbia Turnpike nearly to the south end of the old Long Bridge. Nothing of particular note happened, and all we did was to watch the signalling between the vessels of war then lying off the mouth of the Eastern Branch. We returned about daybreak.

Our people were much amused at about this time to read in the *Virginia Sentinel,* of this city (published in the building which is now the Royal Apartments, on Royal Street) a clipping from the *New York Herald* which ran as follows:

"A Deserter From Alexandria"

"One of the rebel soldiers stationed at Alexandria deserted today and, crossing the river, made his appearance in the camp of the Zouaves.

"He gives a doleful account of affairs in that city and reports great disaffection among the soldiers on account of their being badly fed and clothed.

"He is of the opinion that many of them are only anxious for a good opportunity to desert, and says that Alexandria presents a perfect picture of desolation."

This is hardly consistent with the truth, as we were never so well clothed as we were at that time. We were all wearing our new uniforms, which were of fine quality, and the state was boarding us at the Mansion House, corner of Fairfax and Cameron Streets, to which we were marched three times a day for our meals. Also there was no need for any effort to desert as a soldier desiring to do so had only to remain at home when the time came to leave the city.

In the same issue of the *Herald* there was an account of how two of Ellsworth's Zouaves had crossed over the river in the night, escaping the vigilance of the rebel sentinels, cut down the Jackson flag from the Marshall House, and returned with it safely to their camp on Giesboro Point, on the opposite Maryland shore. This was about as true as the story about the deserters.

As might be guessed from this story the flag on Marshall House was a thorn in the side of the enemy. It was destined to become one of the most famous flags in the history of the war. The proprietor of

Marshall House, Mr. James W. Jackson, had reopened the hotel on January 2, 1861. He came from the adjoining county of Fairfax. He was a strong advocate of secession, and in fact was commissioned as captain by Governor Letcher of Virginia and early in 1861 was enlisting recruits for an artillery company under orders from the governor.

Anticipating the secession of Virginia Captain Jackson had ordered a flag made after the pattern of the "Stars and Bars" of the Confederacy. The order was given to Mrs. John W. Padgett, on North Fairfax Street, who soon reported it finished and ready for the Star of Virginia, which was to be placed in the center of the circle of stars.

Becoming impatient, Jackson would not wait for the adoption or ratification of a secession resolution. Virginia was moving too slowly for him. So on the afternoon of April 17 he hoisted his flag, the Stars and Bars of the Confederacy with the Star of Virginia in the center, over the roof of Marshall House. This was thirty-six days before secession was ratified. I remember standing on the corner opposite and watching the scene and hearing the cheers of the assembled citizens.

While all these things were going on the state was rapidly moving towards a separation from the Union. On the same date as that of the formation of the Southern Confederacy an election was held in our city to select delegates to a convention which was to be held in Richmond to decide the question of secession. The election in Alexandria resulted in the choice of Mr. George William Brent the Union candidate, over Mr. David Funston, advocate of secession, by a vote of 1,119 to 438. However, on April 18, 1861, the state convention passed an ordinance of secession. On May 23, the day before our troops left Alexandria, this ordinance was ratified by the people of the state by the overwhelming majority of more than 130,000. I have in my possession the original election returns of the First Ward, duly signed by the commissioners and clerks. It shows only twelve votes against ratification.

While we were absent at Warrenton an incident occurred which illustrates the uncertain temper of mind of at least one officer as actual hostilities approached.

On May 2 Brigadier General Philip St. George Cocke, commanding the Potomac Department, in which Alexandria was included, with headquarters at Culpeper Court House, received orders from Major General R. E. Lee, commanding the state forces, at Richmond, to place Lieutenant Colonel A. S. Taylor or other experienced officer in command of the troops in and around Alexandria. This was followed by instructions from General Cocke to Taylor to the following effect:

"You will not move the troops out of Alexandria unless pressed by overwhelming and irresistible numbers, and even then you should retire to Manassas Junction to hold that point, assist in obstructing and breaking up the road between that point and Alexandria, harassing the enemy should he attempt to use the road, and not to retire further in the interior unless overpowered and forced, as a last extremity, to so retire.

"You will use your cavalry and infantry in this connection, and, under these orders, which I have full authority from headquarters at Richmond for giving, keep up your communication with the various posts in your rear, so as to call every resource to your aid and support in making a gallant and fighting retreat, should you be forced to it, and can stand at all without danger of uselessly sacrificing your command."

Notwithstanding these instructions Colonel Taylor, while in command, evacuated Alexandria on Sunday, May 5. The movement brought on a considerable correspondence with the Virginia authorities. He was directed to return all the troops to Alexandria immediately, which he did. After an investigation General Cocke on May 7 wired to General Lee at Richmond asking if he should arrest Colonel Taylor for disobedience of orders and unsoldier-like conduct. General Lee replied the next day directing General Cocke not to arrest the colonel but to require explanations from him.

This was done and on May 9 he replied at some length, stating as his reasons for the action, first, that he was occupying an exposed and indefensible position with a large proportion of his troops inefficient and poorly armed; second, that the men were becoming almost useless from home influences; third, that he had apparently reliable information that the government at Washington was planning to occupy the city on May 6 or 7. In support of the third reason he stated that he was enclosing an order obtained secretly by a former employee of the War Department, revealing these plans; no copy of this order, however, was found with the correspondence. In addition, he said that he could more successfully help in breaking up and destroying the roads by retiring to Springfield.

His explanations were evidently not satisfactory and on May 10 he was replaced by Colonel George H. Terrett. The correspondence is chiefly interesting now as showing how poorly armed were the troops in Alexandria. In his letter of May 9 Colonel Taylor says:

"In my command there were two companies of raw Irish recruits, numbering about 120 privates in both, armed with the altered flintlock muskets of 1848, and without cartridges or caps; Captain Devaughn's company (Mount Vernon Guards), 86 privates, armed with the new musket - 52 men without accoutrements and 15 without arms, and very little ammunition; Captain Simpson's company of rifles numbering in all 53, and well armed with the Minie rifle and about nine rounds of ammunition complete; Captain Herbert's company of rifles, numbering 85, rank and file, armed with the Minie rifle, and with an average of five rounds of cartridges and four of caps; Captain Ball's company of cavalry, numbering 40 privates, armed with carbines and sabers and with a very limited amount of ammunition; Captain Powell's company of cavalry numbering about 30, and 22 horses, no arms or equipment of any kind except a few Colt's revolvers."

These detailed statements were no doubt quite in accord with the facts. The troops were really poorly equipped, especially as regards the quality of their arms. The following order is good testimony to that fact:

"Headquarters Virginia Forces,
Richmond, Va., May 2, 1861.

"Gen'l P. St. George Cocke.

"General: The commanding General has today ordered two hundred flint-lock muskets, with fifty rounds of ammunition for each, to be sent without delay to Alexandria for the troops in and around that point. You are requested to notify the officer in command of the fact.

"R. S. Garnett,
Adjutant General."

It was only a short time before leaving the city that the Old Dominion Rifles received 100 Minie rifles, which were captured at Harper's Ferry by our Virginia troops. It was a pretty gun, with a saber-bayonet attachment, and the boys were very proud of their new arms. But we were not allowed the use of them for any length of time as they were replaced by Enfield rifles soon after the Battle of Bull Run.

Colonel Taylor's fears of an invasion by Union troops were somewhat premature, but the tension along the Potomac was tightening. On May 13 Colonel Terrett, then in command at Alexandria, received a report from Captain E. B. Powell, commanding our cavalry outposts, to the effect that his videttes had been fired upon at noon on the preceding Saturday and Sunday. They were stationed at the Aqueduct Bridge, near Georgetown, and the firing came from that city. When they changed their position the firing was renewed on the new position.

The captain said he proceeded with five selected and well armed men to the middle of the bridge, summoned the corporal of the U. S. guard, and demanded an explanation. The corporal said his men had not done the firing; his orders were only to stop supplies and suspicious persons and act on the defensive. Captain Powell then sent a messenger to the mayor of Georgetown, demanding an explanation. He received a reply through the chief of police to the effect that the authorities would punish the offenders if discovered, that the complaint had been brought to the attention of the military commandant, and that all ball cartridges would be taken from the troops quartered in Georgetown. The captain considered the explanation sufficient.

Previous to the occupation of our city by the enemy the steamer *George Page,* a double-ender ferry boat plying between this city and Washington, was seized by our Virginia authorities and held under guard until April 20, when she was sent to Aquia Creek, where she was converted into a gunboat and newly christened the C. S. Steamer *City of Richmond.* The seizure was made by Sergeant Morgan Davis of Kemper's Battery, under orders from Major Corse of the Alexandria Battalion. The boat remained for nearly a year at Aquia Creek, cooperating with the Confederate land forces there. One night late in October, during a storm, she came up the river under cover of the darkness, went first into Quantico Creek, and then crossing over the

29

Potomac close to the Maryland shore threw a number of shells into the camp of the Excelsior Brigade, commanded by General Sickles. The Union troops were forced to take a position farther inland. The Federal authorities were apprehensive of a Confederate landing in Maryland. In March, 1862, when the Confederate forces retired to the line of the Rappahannock River, the guns were removed and the boat was burned at Aquia Creek.

On May 20, 1861, the Confederate Congress, then in session at Montgomery, Alabama, resolved that the seat of government of the Confederate States should be transferred to Richmond, and that the Congress should adjourn to meet there on July 20. It had already become evident that Virginia would be the battleground of the coming struggle, and it was desirable, therefore, that the Confederate Government should have its headquarters in that state.

On Thursday, May 23, the day before our departure from the city, several large U. S. Ocean Mail steamers, one of them the *Cahawba* as I read its name, passed up the river with several thousand soldiers aboard, going to reinforce the army in Washington. They jeered us as they passed.

CHAPTER V

OFF TO THE CONFLICT

OUR daily practice of guard duty and details was kept up until the eventful 24th of May. It was about 2 o'clock in the morning when the commander of this post, Colonel George H. Terrett, formerly of the U. S. Marine Corps, was informed by our pickets that the enemy were crossing the Chain and Long Bridges between Alexandria and Washington.

At about 4 o'clock in the morning our pickets on the water front escorted in an officer (a Lieutenant Lowery) bearing a flag of truce. He had landed from the gunboat *Pawnee* with orders for the evacuation or surrender of the city. He was informed that we would evacuate, and we were given until 9 o'clock to do so. Notwithstanding this agreement, long before 9 o'clock troops numbering more than 5,000, including infantry, cavalry, and artillery, were crossing the country in an effort to cut off and capture our force. Troops had also landed from a number of transports in front of the city and had driven in our pickets stationed there.

At this time Colonel Terrett's headquarters were at the southeast corner of Prince and St. Asaph Streets. The guard house at which all the companies were to assemble in case of an alarm was at the Lyceum Hall, at the southwest corner of Washington and Streets. Guard mount was held each morning at 8 o'clock, on the east side of Washington Street, the formation extending from the corner up Prince Street as far down as the First Baptist Church.

When the different companies had reached this point on the morning of May 24 the battalion was formed and was ordered to take the Duke Street road leading in the direction of Manassas. The morning of the evacuation found the Old Dominion Rifles at their quarters, Peyton's Grove, which was located directly in front of the present Alexandria High School building. Through a misunderstanding, our company did not leave their quarters as early as the other companies.

Up to this time but little ammunition had been issued to the men. After forming line, Captain Herbert proceeded to give out the cartridges. Passing down the line he gave to each man two rounds of ammunition and ordered us to load our rifles. There were not enough cartridges to go around the third time, and for want of a cartridge box I had to put my extra cartridge in my pocket. That will give an idea of the state of our supply and equipment at that date.

While we were marching down King Street on our way to the appointed place of assembly two small boys, who were standing on the southeast corner at Patrick Street, called to Captain Herbert and told him that Mr. Jackson had been shot at Marshall House. Looking down King Street we could see the crowd assembled at Marshall House. On being questioned the boys said that the other companies had marched out Duke Street. We then marched south on Patrick Street to Duke, finally overtaking the main body on the road at some distance from the city.

During the morning we halted once when a number of horsemen appeared approaching us in the rear. We prepared to repulse what we thought was a squadron of Union cavalry in pursuit, but the riders turned out to be straggling cavalry of our own forces making its escape. Nothing more of note occurred until we halted some incoming trains about two miles out. We boarded them and were carried to Manassas, a railway station about twenty-seven miles from Alexandria, reaching there at about 1 o'clock p. m. Two companies (G and I) of our command were left along the road to burn the railroad bridges. We found encamped at Manassas several thousand troops from various states.

The men who left Alexandria on May 24 were all volunteers and residents of the city. They numbered over 700, as follows: Company A, 130; Company E, 124; Company G, 77; Company H, 114; Company I, 57; total infantry, 502. Kemper's Alexandria Artillery had 117 men, cavalry troops numbered 45, and Alexandrians with other commands numbered 58, a grand total of 722 men. Truly that was a goodly contribution from a city which had a population, according to the census of the year before, of 12,652, white and colored. The number given includes only troops from Alexandria itself and not those in the Washington and other outside companies.

The commander of the Alexandria Battalion at the time of its departure from the city was Major Montgomery D. Corse. Under him the officers of the various companies were as follows:[**]

Company A: Captain, Morton Marye; First Lieutenant, A.J. Humphries; Second Lieutenants, W. W. Smith and P.B. Hooe; First Sergeant, Charles J. Wise.

Company E: Captain, Samuel H. Devaughn; First Lieutenant, William H. Smith; Second Lieutenants, W. W. Allen and Charles Javins; First Sergeant, John T. Devaughn.

Company G: Captain, James E. Towson; First Lieutenant, W. H. Kemper; Second Lieutenants, Robert F. Knox and Charles W. Wattles; First Sergeant, James W. Ivors.

Company H: Captain, Arthur Herbert; First Lieutenant, William H. Fowle, Jr.; Second Lieutenants, Douglass F. Forrest and W. W. Zimmerman; First Sergeant, Arthur C. Kell.

Company I: Captain, S. W. Prestman; First Lieutenant, Raymond Fairfax; Second Lieutenant, H. S. Wallace; First Sergeant, John S. Hart.

Kemper's Battery: Captain, Delaware Kemper; Lieutenants, David L. Smoot, W. D. Stuart, Richard H. Bayliss, and William H. Kemper; First Sergeant, E. Samuel Duffey.

News of our retirement from Alexandria was flashed to General Lee by telegraph by Henry Dangerfield soon after our arrival at Manassas. He announced that five thousand Federal troops had entered the city at 5 o'clock in the morning, that our troops had retired in good order just ahead of the enemy, and that bridges on the railway had been burned as far as Fairfax Station. A report dated May 24 indicates that the movement on the part of the enemy took the Confederate authorities to a certain extent by surprise:

"Richmond, Va.,
May 24, 1861.

"L. P. Walker,
        Secretary of War:

[**]The muster roll of these companies is given in the
Appendix.

"Telegraph office here has information from Manassas junction via Lynchburg, of the occupation of Alexandria this morning by 5,000 Federal troops. Confirmatory of this information is the fact that there are three distinct wires hence to Alexandria, and no answer can be had from the latter office.

"General Lee is much mortified, admits he was unprepared, having only 600 troops in Alexandria.

> "Signed   W. G. Duncan."

On the same day General Cocke, at Culpeper Court House, officially reported a message from General Bonham, at Manassas, to the effect that Alexandria was taken and that Colonel Terrett was at Manassas with his Alexandria troops.

Colonel Terrett telegraphed to General Lee from Manassas that the Alexandria forces retreated in good order, their rear guard in sight of, and within two hundred yards of, the advance guard of the enemy. On May 28 he made the following report:

> "Manassas Junction, Camp Pickens,
>
> May 28, 1861.

"Sir: In obedience to instructions from Headquarters at this date, in regard to the capture of Captain Ball and his troop, I have to report that on the morning of the 24th inst., about 1 :30 o'clock, Captain Ball came to my quarters and reported that one of the videttes, stationed at the Chain Bridge, about three miles west of Georgetown, D. C., had informed him that a squadron of cavalry had crossed over to the Virginia shore. I immediately ordered my command, under arms, to await further orders.

"About 5:30 a. m. an officer was sent from the steamer *Pawnee*, Northern Navy, to inform me that an overwhelming force was about entering the city of Alexandria, and it would be madness to resist, and that I would have until 9 a. m. to evacuate or surrender. I then ordered the troops under my command to assemble at the place designated by me on assuming command in Alexandria, that I might either resist or fall back, as circumstances might require.

"As soon as the troops were formed, which was promptly done, I repaired to the command, and then, ascertaining that the enemy were entering the city by Washington Street, and that several steamers had been placed so that their guns could command many of the principal streets, I ordered the command to march and proceeded out of the city by Duke Street.

"Captain Ball accompanied me as far as his quarters, a little west of the railroad depot, where he halted, and I proceeded to the cars, which were about a half-mile from the depot, where I had ordered them to be stopped. From orders given before marching out of the city, the cavalry was to follow me in my rear for the purpose of giving me information in regard to the movements of the enemy. Captain Powell followed my instructions, and why Captain Ball did not I am unable to report.

"George H. Terrett,
"Colonel Com'd'g, Alexandria, Va."

In his report on the occupation of the city Major General Charles W. Sanford, U. S. A., states that the capture of Captain W. D. Ball and thirty-five men of the Fairfax Cavalry was made by Sherman's battery of light artillery.

The Union telegram to Washington announcing the occupation of the city was sent shortly after the landing of the troops. It also told of the capture of the cavalry troop:

"Alexandria, Va.,
May 24, 1861.

"Alexandria is ours. One company, Captain Ball, mounted, thirty-five men and thirty-five horses, captured. I regret to say Colonel Ellsworth has been shot by a person in a house.

"Yours,

O. B. Willcox, Colonel."

"To General Mansfield."

According to the report of Major General of Volunteers S. P. Heintzelman, the Federal troops were ordered on May 23 to be ready to march at a moment's notice. At 9 p. m. orders were sent directing them to march to the Washington end of the Long Bridge. At 2 a. m. they were to enter on the bridge, and precisely at that hour the troops advanced, the Twelfth New York Regiment leading the way. Other troops crossing by the Long Bridge were the Seventh and Twenty-fifth New York and the Third New Jersey Regiments, with one company of cavalry and one battery of artillery, and the First Michigan Regiment, with pioneers, one company of cavalry, and one battery of artillery.

Troops crossing by the Aqueduct were the Fifth, Fourteenth, Twenty-eighth, and Sixty-ninth New York Regiments, with one company of cavalry and one battery of artillery.

The First Michigan Regiment, under Colonel Willcox, was ordered to march direct to Alexandria and to unite there with the Eleventh New York (the "Ellsworth Fire Zouaves"), under Colonel Ellsworth, and occupy the city. The latter regiment came by steamer from its encampment on the Potomac, below the Eastern Branch, and was landed on the wharves of Alexandria under the guns of the gunboat *Pawnee*.

According to Major General Heintzelman's report in regard to the movement of troops on the 23rd, the occupation of Alexandria was not included in the original plan, but this part of the plan was changed before the troops began their march.

The Long Bridge, over which the greater portion of the invading troops crossed in their advance into Virginia, was an old wooden structure, located less than seventy-five yards east of the present Pennsylvania Railroad bridge. The land approach to the Virginia end of the old bridge is all that remains of it. The Aqueduct Bridge was directly at Georgetown and was the property of the Alexandria Canal Company, which received a charter from Congress in 1830. At the beginning of the war it was taken over by the Federal authorities and used for military purposes. It was over this bridge that most of the wounded were conveyed after the rout of the Federal troops at Bull Run, and after that it was used mostly for the crossing of the Union wounded from the battlefields of Virginia.

It is said that when the Federal troops under General McDowell crossed over into Virginia from Washington the bands were playing and the soldiers singing, "John Brown's soul goes marching on." Under the inspiration of that song they carried out John Brown's mission in Virginia on many occasions when opportunity offered.

Besides the casualties mentioned one other death resulted from the occupation of Alexandria on May 24. During the Presidential campaign one of the contending political parties had erected a flag pole on the southeast corner of Cameron and Royal Streets. This was standing on the morning of our evacuation, but it had not been used for several days is it was minus the halyards. During the morning a sailor from one of the warships in front of the city was ordered to climb the pole and adjust the cords. Before he reached the top he lost his hold and fell to the sidewalk and was instantly killed.

The tragedy which occurred at Marshall House when the city was evacuated has become famous in history. As stated, it was enacted while the main body of our troops was marching out and while my company was marching down King Street, the occupation of the city at that hour being in direct violation of the agreement between Colonel Terrett and the officer bearing the flag of truce that we were to have until 9 o'clock to evacuate.

The details of what occurred at the Marshall House on that morning were given by one of our reliable citizens, Mr. Joseph L. Padgett, before the R. E. Lee Camp of this city. Mr. Padgett was an eyewitness of the whole affair.

He said that he was standing on the southeast corner of King and Fairfax Streets when William Morrill, of the Alexandria Riflemen, who was our picket at the foot of Cameron Street, came running up and told him that the Union troops were landing on the river front. Soon after, the head of the New York Eleventh Regiment (the "Fire Zouaves"), recruited only that year from among the volunteer firemen of New York by Colonel Elmer E. Ellsworth, who was only twenty-four years of age, came marching up Cameron Street. They turned south into Fairfax and then went up King to the Marshall House. Mr. Padgett followed them on the sidewalk.

It was reported that Ellsworth was selected to lead the advance into Alexandria because he had promised the President's wife that if he should be accorded the privilege he would bring her the flag that was flying over the Marshall House as a trophy.

The colonel, with a sergeant and six or eight men, entered the hotel just as the old colored porter was opening the office. Placing a guard at the door with orders to allow no one to enter he went upstairs on the way to the roof.

Mr. Padgett, who was an intimate friend of the proprietor, had entered before the order was given. He followed the colonel and his men and had reached the foot of the stairs leading to the third floor when he was ordered by one of the guards not to come any farther. Ellsworth succeeded in getting the flag and was on his way down when Jackson, the proprietor, in his night clothes, came from his room on the second floor out into the hallway. Seeing Mr. Padgett he asked what all the noise was about and was told that the Yankees were out on the roof after his flag.

Stepping quickly back into his room where his wife lay sleeping he reached behind the door and got his double-barrelled shot-gun and ran half-way up the stairs to a landing where he waited for Ellsworth and his men, who were descending. As the colonel reached the head of the stairs Jackson fired and killed him. Immediately afterwards he himself fell, being shot by Sergeant Brownell of the New York regiment.

Jackson had evidently anticipated that someone would try to lower his flag or had expected trouble of some kind, as he had requested his friend Mr. James W. Graham, to whom he had loaned his shot-gun a few days before, to return it as he might have need for it. Mr. Graham returned the gun on the day before the tragedy, telling him that it was already loaded. It is now in the National Museum at Washington.

Jackson had also borrowed a little cannon, well known to many of our citizens as the "Coon Killer," which was the property of Mr. John A. Rudd and was used to fire salutes on public occasions. Jackson placed this gun in his yard, under a porch, the muzzle pointing towards the King Street entrance of the hotel and commanding the main hall way. He had taken these precautions to defend his property, as he had heard threats that his flag would be pulled down. This gun was overlooked in the excitement within the building. I am told that its owner succeeded in getting it and that he removed it from the wheels, carried it across the street, and threw it down a well, covering it with a lot of rubbish. It remained there during the entire war, after which it was recovered and used again for its original purpose.

An hour or two after the deaths of Jackson and Ellsworth the acting coroner of the county, Mr. James A. English, held an inquest over Jackson's body. The jury, after being sworn and after hearing the evidence, rendered the following verdict:

"That the said James W. Jackson came to his death; upon their oaths they do say, that he was killed by an armed body of Federal troops when in defence of his home and his private rights.

"In witness thereof the said coroner and jurors herewith set their hands, this 24th day of May, 1861."

The verdict was signed by James A. English, Justice of the Peace; George L. Deeton, Foreman; and John Cogan, J. C. Engelbrecht, Elijah Horseman, Charles L. Neale, Wesley Avery, John Jones, Christopher W. Deeton, Joseph Padgett, Jr., John L. Smith, W. L. Simpson, and John Formshil.

During the same day the body of Colonel Ellsworth was conveyed to Washington on the steamer *James Guy*. Because of his popularity many of the bells in that city were tolled on the arrival of the body.

CHAPTER VI

IN CAMP AT MANASSAS

ON the day after our arrival at Manassas General M. L. Bonham, commanding that post, telegraphed to General Lee at Richmond that "the Alexandria troops are here without cooking utensils, and many without arms." He asked that cooking utensils and other camp equipage for 600 men be sent to the quartermaster there.

We passed Friday and Saturday quietly after our arrival. At night the men slept for the first time on the ground, although a few found quarters in some empty freight cars standing on the track nearby. A few days later a part of our company was installed in frame buildings, made of rough boards hastily put together, with both ends open. On either side were bunks holding two persons each.

As might be expected there was a certain amount of nervousness among these raw troops. On Sunday we were called to arms by our pickets, who mistook the movements of our men for those of the enemy. However, quiet was soon restored. There was another false alarm the next day, when a report that the enemy was advancing on Fairfax Court House had us again in line. But we soon returned to our quarters.

This second alarm caught several of us in a predicament. When we had hurriedly left our homes many of us had brought away only one suit of underwear, which was the one we had on. We were washing these clothes at a little stream, and had hung them on some bushes to dry, meanwhile lolling around in the shade, when the "long roll" was sounded. We hastily pulled on our outer clothing and in that state fell in line. Fortunately on our return we found our clothes still on the bushes and ready to be put on.

Troops were arriving on every train. They were immediately detrained and sent off to camps at some distance from us. General Lee, who on May 10 had been assigned command of all the troops serving in Virginia, paid a visit to us here at Manassas.

On May 31 a lady came out from Alexandria bringing the flag of the Alexandria Riflemen, which had been left behind on the morning of our departure.

On June 1 the Warrenton Rifles (Company K of the Seventeenth Virginia Infantry), commanded by Captain John Q. Marr, who were stationed at Fairfax Court House, about thirteen miles below in the direction of Alexandria, were attacked by a body of Union cavalry Second U.S. Regulars) under the command of Lieutenant Charles H. Tompkins. The enemy was repulsed with loss, but the Rifles lost their captain, who was killed. We learned afterwards that Lieutenant Tompkins was seriously wounded in this action.

On the same date as this brush with the enemy, June 1, General P. G. T. Beauregard, who was to assume command of the troops assembling at this point, arrived in camp. On the 8th of June Governor Letcher issued a proclamation transferring all Virginia troops, ordnance, stores, etc., to the Confederate States. The total strength in men was 40,000, with 115 guns.

A few days after our arrival at Manassas I was for the first time detailed to work on the breastworks with the pick and shovel. It was a novel treat for one who had never before handled either implement - although in that respect, it is almost needless to say, I had lots of company.

Our chaplain, the Rev. George H. Norton, was preaching regularly to the soldiers in the camp, and always to large and attentive audiences.

The Seventeenth Virginia Regiment of Infantry was formed on June 10. It was composed of the following companies:
Company A, Alexandria Riflemen; Captain, Morton Marye.
Company B, Warren Rifles; Captain, R. H. Simpson.
Company C, Loudoun Guards; Captain, C. B. Tebbs.
Company D, Fairfax Rifles; Captain, William H. Dulaney.
Company E, Mount Vernon Guards; Captain, S. H. Devaughn.
Company F, Prince William Rifles; Captain, G. S. Hamilton.
Company G, Emmett Guards; Captain, James E. Towson.
Company H, Old Dominion Rifles; Captain, Arthur Herbert.
Company I, O'Connell Guards; Captain, S. W. Prestman.
Company K, Warrenton Rifles; Captain, B. H. Shackelford.
Major M. B. Corse was made colonel, William Munford was

chosen as lieutenant colonel, and George William Brent was made major. Other appointments were: Surgeon, Dr. M. M. Lewis; assistant surgeon, Harold Snowden; adjutant, A. D. Humphreys of Company A; sergeant major, W. W. Athey of the Loudoun Guards; hospital steward, W. C. Milburn of Company A. The last-named held his position throughout the entire war.

Soon after the regiment was formed, as required by the army regulations, it underwent a medical examination. This was a mere matter of form with us. All we had to do was to answer "Yes" when the question was put to each of us, "Are you sound in wind and limb?" As we were all anxious to pass the answer was the same from all of us.

The regiment was attached to the Fourth Brigade of the Army of the Potomac, which brigade was commanded by Brigadier General James Longstreet, and was composed of the First, Eleventh, and Seventeenth Virginia Regiments of Infantry. General Longstreet assumed command of his brigade on July 2, and on July 6 we were marched out formed as a brigade and put through the first evolution of the line. These brigade drills were kept up until the advance of McDowell's army, and they were said to be the only brigade drills held in our army. They were never held after the First Battle of Manassas, much to the delight of the men, for they were both tiresome and tedious affairs.

I recall a little incident at one of these drills which for a while caused all the boys of Company H to carry their heads high. At the finish of the drill General Longstreet requested that our company remain on the field and drill before him. Needless to say, we did it in great style, and we were duly complimented.

From the time of the organization of the company to its assignment as Company H of the regiment we had drilled to the sound of a bugle. As bugler we had a well-known character of our city who prided himself very much on his military appearance in his stunning uniform and who was troubled somewhat with what is now termed the "big head." Every day at the early morning call he used to place his bugle at the ear of any sleeping form within reach and give the drowsy soldier the full benefit of the blast. One morning he put his lips to the mouthpiece of the bugle and found that two could play at the game of practical jokes. His instrument had been filled with all kinds of trash, to his supreme disgust. It was his last bugle call for Company H, as he was transferred on that same day to a cavalry troop.

On June 16 a section of Kemper's Alexandria Battery accompanied the First South Carolina Infantry on a reconnaissance to Dranesville, Fairfax County. When returning the next day they heard the whistle of an approaching train. Colonel Maxcy Gregg, commanding the force, placed the guns of the battery on a hill at Vienna, a station on the Alexandria and Loudoun Railroad. This was about 6 o'clock p. m. As the train came around the curve Kemper opened on it with a rapid fire from his guns, badly damaging it and causing the First Ohio Regiment, under Brigadier General Schenck, to alight from it and beat a hasty retreat. Kemper destroyed one passenger and five platform cars, captured some arms, and killed and wounded numbers of the enemy, without loss to our side.

According to an account of the affair written by a Northern reporter for his paper, General Schenck "had novel notions of warfare and intended to carry on operations in a free and easy style. So, embarking two or three Ohio regiments on a long train, with two field pieces, he proceeded down the railroad, the engine being in the rear of the train. Colonel Maxcy Gregg * * * prepared to give them a warm reception. He placed two of Kemper's guns on a wooded eminence commanding a long curve in the road. The train leisurely approached, with Schenck and his officers enjoying themselves with champagne and cigars, unconscious of danger. As the train entered the curve mentioned the guns of the Confederates opened with destructive effect. Seven cars were detached from the train and smashed to pieces and many of the occupants were killed and wounded."

Colonel Gregg, in his report of the affair, said that Captain Del Kemper's command showed great ardor, combined with discipline, and the skill of Captain Kemper and Lieutenant Stuart in managing the guns left nothing to be desired. (Kemper on this occasion had only two guns and thirty-four men.) General Schenck in his report said that the two pieces of Confederate artillery "were fired so rapidly they must have been managed by skillful artillerists."

During our stay at this Manassas camp, called "Camp Pickens" after the Governor of South Carolina, details were made daily for many other purposes than guard duty, and the troops had but few idle moments.

Soon after the regiment was organized we were given tents and went regularly into camp life. It was here at Manassas that we really received our first lessons in the life of a soldier. It is amusing to us now to think of the follies we committed in the early days of the war, of how we got ourselves up, of the outfit with which we fitted ourselves and which was so soon to be cast aside as utterly worthless. Very soon we found out the inconvenience of having too much luggage. Our first march made us realize that we must reduce ourselves to the lightest marching trim, and the great cumbersome knapsack, heavily loaded with everything we thought a soldier might need, soon became a thing of the past.

Overcoats were to a great extent discarded and the one blanket was made to serve in its place. When this was to be carried it was rolled lengthwise in a rubber cloth (with which nearly every soldier was supplied through captured goods), tied together at the ends, and worn over one shoulder, with the ends coming under the arm on the other side. Woolen underwear was also cast aside, as ordinary cotton goods were found to be best for cleanliness and general wear.

We had to learn how to prepare our quarters and to form cooking messes - and at first, I can assure you, they were really "messes!" Our company at first was divided into three messes and men were selected as cooks, being relieved from other camp duties while acting in that capacity. They knew no more about cooking than a man who had never seen a frying pan or skillet, and soon the men rebelled and swore they would eat no more of the rations cooked by these novices. The biscuits were compared to solid shot, and the flapjacks or cakes were almost tough enough to half-sole shoes with. On the day of the final break-up of that system of messes the boys nailed several of these flapjacks to the trees. Some of them said that when they passed the camp more than a year later these cakes still remained nailed to the trees, in spite of all the storms and tempests to which they had been subjected. Truly they were tough, and how we managed to live after eating them is a mystery to this day.

Eventually we were allowed to form messes to suit ourselves. The men became contented with this system, and it continued throughout the war. My own mess was composed of six comrades - D. H. Appich, W. J. Hall, Edgar Warfield, B. C. White, Jonah W. Baldwin, and E. F. Baldwin. We planned things so that two could do the cooking, while the other four were to keep them supplied with water and fuel, taking turns at these tasks. While in camp we were to relieve them of all other duties, such as guard and picket.

As a matter of course there had to be one man in the mess who would try in every way to evade work, putting off until the last minute the job of bringing water or wood in the hope that neither would be needed for that day. More than once during our stay in camp would the water container be emptied when he was out of sight, so that he would be compelled to go for more no matter what the weather or the distance he had to travel.

One night when I was on guard duty I made the usual call "Lights out!" when "Taps" was sounded, but the occupants of a tent in Company A paid no heed. I knew they were having a quiet game of cards, and I thought I would let them play their hand out.

I waited a while, but when they kept on playing I again called, in a very sharp voice, "Lights out in Company A!" An answer came back inviting me to "go to h--." Not being able to leave my post to obey such an order, I called, "Sergeant of the Guard, Post No. 5!" Then the lights went out very promptly. When I explained the matter to the sergeant and his guard, we went over to the row of tents of Company A and found the occupants of every tent apparently sound asleep and snoring to beat the band. In the darkness I was unable to designate the tent, so the laugh was on me.

Many were the tricks the boys worked to smuggle liquor into camp. Once while I was talking to one of the camp sentries on duty a soldier carrying a coffee pot came up on his way into camp. When the guard asked him what he had in the pot he said he had milk, at the same time tilting the pot enough to cause milk to flow from the spout. This satisfied the guard and the soldier passed on. Of course the pot was filled with whiskey. The owner had simply corked the lower end of the spout and filled the spout itself with milk.

At another time five men, fully equipped and apparently on duty, passed out of camp. Returning later, they were passed in. The guard did not know until several days had passed that each gun barrel was filled to the muzzle with liquor.

CHAPTER VII

FIRST BATTLE OF MANASSAS

ON the morning of July 17th I was detailed, along with a large number of others, with Major Williamson, an engineer officer, to help clear the ground where trees had been felled in front of some earthworks which had been built in sight of our camp. While we were working the sound of the long roll was heard throughout the various camps. Curious to know the cause, we stopped work and sent one of our number, Albion Hurdle, over to the camp to learn what was up. In a few moments he appeared on the edge of the camp and waved to us to come in. We did so on the run, and found the regiment in line ready to move off. We began getting ourselves ready to fall in, but the regiment marched off without us. But we were soon able to overtake it, learning that it was on its way to Bull Run and that the enemy was advancing upon us, having left Washington on the night before.

Our advanced brigade, under General Bonham, was stationed at Fairfax Court House. Following previous instructions it began its withdrawal and effected the movement with complete success, being within our lines during the day and night of the 17th.

It was evident that the great conflict toward which our thoughts had turned for so long was at last upon us. On that same day, July 17, General Beauregard issued an order to the troops in which he said:

"The General Commanding the Army of the Potomac announces to his command that at length the enemy have advanced to subjugate a sovereign state, and to impose upon a free people an odious government. Notwithstanding their numerical superiority they can be repelled, and the General Commanding relies confidently on his command to do it, and to drive the invader back beyond his intrenched line. To do this the highest order of coolness, individual intelligence, and obedience on the part of each officer and man are essential.

"Great reliance will be placed on the bayonet at the proper juncture, but above all it is enjoined on officers and men to withhold their fire until directed. The superior intelligence of the individual members of this command should in this respect compensate for the want of a veteran, long trained soldiery. In firing, each man should take aim and never discharge his piece without a distinct object in view."

When we arrived at Bull Run our line of battle was extended from Union Mills, on our right, to the Stone Bridge on our extreme left, a distance of seven or eight miles. Bull Run is a small stream rising in the neighborhood of Aldie and winding about amid fields and roads until it falls into the Occoquan. It runs between Centreville and Manassas, about three miles from each place. Our center was at Mitchell's Ford, on the main road from Centreville to Manassas, and our position covered Blackburn's Ford, which is between Mitchell's and McLean's Fords and about one half mile from each. My company was directly at the fording place at Blackburn's Ford.

Our position was described in General Beauregard's report of the battle at this point as follows:

"The northern bank of the stream in front of us rises with a steep slope at least fifty feet above the level of the water, leaving a narrow berme in front of the ford of some twenty yards. The ridge formed for the enemy an admirable natural parapet, behind which they could and did approach under shelter in heavy force, within less than one hundred yards of our line. The southern shore was almost a plain, raised but a few feet above the water, about five or six feet for several hundred yards. I also desire to place on record that on the 18th of July not one yard of intrenchments nor one rifle pit sheltered the men at Blackburn's Ford. The officers and men, with rare exception, were on that day for the first time under fire, and, taking and maintaining every position ordered, cannot be too much commended for their soldierly behavior."

Such was our position at Blackburn's Ford on the morning of Thursday, July 18, when the first attack of the Union forces was made. It was about 1 o'clock when we heard the bugle call of the enemy for their skirmishers to advance. Not more than a minute or two later their whole line showed up and made their first effort to cross the stream, directly in front of us, and were handsomely repulsed by the First and Seventeenth Virginia Regiments and four companies of the Eleventh (Lynchburg) Regiment.

They made three attempts to force the passage, the last with increased force and determination, but were driven back each time. Then the Alexandria Riflemen, Company A, were ordered to cross the stream and clear the enemy from the ford, which they did. At the close of this day's fight we were relieved just before dark by the Seventh Louisiana Regiment.

During the entire fight General Longstreet, mounted, remained only a few yards in the rear of our company. Before the action began he heard one of the boys asking another, "I wonder what they expect us to do here?" and replied that he expected us to keep the enemy from crossing the run if that should be attempted. We told him we would, and we did. In his general orders after the fight General Longstreet complimented Colonel Corse, Lieutenant Colonel Munford, Major Brent, and Surgeon Snowden, and the regiment, for the coolness and bravery displayed on that day.

In this fight of the 18th we had assigned to us two guns of the famous Washington Artillery of New Orleans (Walton's battery) and I had the pleasure of seeing a schoolmate of mine, Sam Boush, in action, he being a member of that company. The movements of a battery while in action were something entirely new to us, and we watched them with a great deal of interest. The horses having been sent to the rear, the guns were maneuvered by hand to different parts of the field whenever the enemy would get their range.

One incident of this fight was of the deepest personal interest to me. When Company A crossed the stream, as related, my father, who was a member of it, waved and called to me as he passed my company, which was still in its original position at the ford. Company A soon became hotly engaged. Deploying as skirmishers they came in contact with the First Massachusetts Regiment and my father came into close quarters with one of the enemy. As his gun was empty and he had no time to reload, he immediately closed in and crossed bayonets with his foe.

The Yankee proved to be a powerful man, weighing about 180 pounds, and he was an expert with his gun. My father weighed some 225 pounds and was naturally rather slow in his movements. After a number of passes, the Yankee succeeded in disarming his opponent by striking him on the shoulder with the butt of his gun, causing my father to drop his own rifle. By turning quickly he caught his foe by the throat and the Yankee in turn dropped his gun. Then the real struggle began. For a few minutes there was a regular rough-and-tumble fist fight, during which the two men rolled down an embankment into a muddy stream that flowed from a spring near the top of the hill. It is difficult to say how the fight would have ended had not Private Edwards of Company C come to my father's assistance.

The two men were so covered with mud that they could hardly be distinguished one from the other. The prisoner was taken to General Longstreet, who was sitting on his horse just in rear of the line. He complimented father on bringing in the first prisoner and suggested that he go and get another.

After the last repulse of the enemy one of their troops, evidently bewildered, appeared on the bank of the stream opposite us. He was dressed in gray - like us, many of the Northern troops were still wearing the uniforms their companies wore before entering the service - and we were uncertain which army he belonged to. Many guns were aimed at him, when Lieutenant Forrest, of my Company, ordered us not to fire until we were sure of our man.

"Who are you, where are you from?" the Lieutenant called over to him.

Raising his gun and arms above his head, the man shouted back: "Union, Massachusetts, from Washington."

They were his last words, as a volley from our side ended his earthly career,

A Northern writer, giving an account of the fight of the 18th at Blackburn's Ford, says:

"It greatly encouraged the Confederates and had a depressing effect upon McDowell's army. The regiments which suffered most were completely demoralized."

The troops on the Union side engaged in this fight at Blackburn's Ford (which is known as the Battle of Bull Run, the fight on the 21st being known as the First Manassas) belonged to Tyler's Division and consisted of Richardson's Brigade, composed of the Second and Third Michigan Regiments, the First Massachusetts, and the Twelfth New York, and a section of twenty-pounder rifled guns of the

Second Artillery.

In his lengthy report made ten days after the fight General Richardson says that "the Twelfth New York, in an effort to obey my order to charge the position held by the Seventeenth Virginia Regiment, broke and was only rallied in the woods some mile and a half in the rear" and that "the artillery fire was continued from 3:15 until 4 o'clock, firing in that time 415 shots."

The countersign used on Thursday was "Sumpter" and on Friday "Our Homes."

The effect of Thursday's fight at Blackburn's Ford was to satisfy the enemy that he could not force a passage across Bull Run on our right, in face of our troops. The alternative, as McDowell said in his report, was therefore to turn the extreme left of our position. This led the enemy into the flank movement of July 21, the "Battle of Manassas."

On the morning of Saturday, the 20th, my company returned to its former position at Blackburn's Ford. There we spent the day and the night, waiting for the struggle of the morrow and listening to the sounds of the moving of the enemy's artillery and wagon trains, and the sound of his drums and bugles and the commands of the officers, all of which could be distinctly heard on the quiet night.

Before daylight on the morning of Sunday, the 21st, my company, the Old Dominion Rifles, was ordered across the run as skirmishers. We advanced on our hands and knees in the direction of the enemy, several hundred yards from our supports, where we lay for some hours under the shelling of Ayre's battery, Company E, Third Artillery of U. S. Regulars. This battery had six guns, and a little later two twenty-pound rifle guns under Lieutenant Benjamin were added.

We were watching and reporting the movements of the enemy to the general when we were discovered by the enemy, who made an effort to cut us off from the main body and capture our entire company by sending a force around our right. They succeeded in getting in the rear of our advanced line, which was under the command of Captain Arthur Herbert, and came in contact with the reserve pickets under Lieutenant Fowle, of which I happened to be one. They were discovered by Arthur Lovelace, who was on the extreme right of our reserve line. He gave the alarm and they were quickly driven out of the woods and put to flight. Then their batteries, which had been shelling over our heads at the main line, opened on us with grape and canister and we were ordered back to our position in line.

We had one man killed, Dennis McDermott, and three wounded in this fight. Except for this little skirmish of Company H the regiment took no active part in the battle of Sunday but only in the pursuit. At one time in the morning the regiment was ordered to cross the ford and did so promptly, forming in column at the head of the ravine on the enemy's bank, near their batteries. Shot and shell were incessantly poured over their heads, but without any damage. Under orders the regiment present retired to its original position.

Such is the brief outline of our part in the Battle of First Manassas. A more detailed account was contained in a letter from an officer of the Old Dominion Rifles to a member of his family then living in Richmond, and it afterwards found its way into one of the Richmond papers. It has many vivid personal touches and is worth reproducing here:

"Saturday night was spent in watching. The enemy's bugles, his drums, the rumble of his baggage trains and artillery, not only these but the very words of command, were distinctly audible in the silent night.

"The next morning, partly refreshed, we were ordered over the ford (Bull Run) as scouts in that direction. I was creeping over the field when the enemy threw a shell at my party which exploded just in advance of us. Here we passed a body, one of the Massachusetts slain (shot the day before), blackened and ghastly.

"After a few hours we were ordered to our reserve and, without breakfast, to deploy as skirmishers. The first reserve had been left in charge of Willie Fowle. I led the second further on, while the captain placed himself in the skirt of the wood, having established a line of sentries. Here he watched the enemy's batteries, and would report their movements to the general.

"Becoming anxious about him I left my reserve under Lieutenant Zimmerman and advanced to the spot. The captain said, "Doug, I am awfully sleepy and will just take a nap if you will watch those fellows there." I cheerfully acquiesced and relieved Jordan, one of our men, who was the actual lookout at the fence. Here I lay on my face, my time pleasantly occupied with the proceedings at the batteries, the ceaseless explosions of the guns and the rattle of musketry from the great fight below (above) being in strong contrast with the quiet scenery of mountain and valleys.

"I unclasped my sword belt and yielded myself to the seductions of the scene, and was startled from my almost reverie by the cry of Lovelace, one of my men posted on the right:

"Look out, Lieutenant! Here they are!"

Looking around I saw their skirmishers within about thirty yards, with their pieces at a ready and advancing just as sportsmen approach a covey of partridges. I shouted to the captain and we dashed into the woods. I then asked him if we should fight them. He said he "reckoned we had." I then yelled to the boys, "Come on, Old Dominions! Now's your chance, now's the chance you've waited for!" This shout of mine was heard by our forces on the other side of the run. The boys say I said, "Isn't this glorious!" but I don't remember. On came the boys, I led them, pointed out the Yankees, and we drove them out of the woods and completely put them to flight.

"As we drove them into the field the enemy's battery, about four hundred yards off, opened on us with grape and canister and we ordered a retreat, not, however, before our men returned it, firing right at the gun, wounding, as I have since learned from a prisoner, several of their men.

"We were exposed nearly a half mile without support. The enemy had our range completely and we were in great peril, the balls whizzing and humming all around us. Fowle, who had advanced his reserve and behaved with great coolness, says the line of skirmishers extended a long way and intended to cut us off. But we gave a yell, and as I have said drove them off. A- was too slow in retreat, even after he had given the order. I had to turn back twice to look for him. How the balls rattled! Every man would sometimes have to get behind a tree to escape the 'dreadful storm'.

"McDermott, one of our men, was killed by a grape shot. On yesterday I buried him. He had lain out all night and our eyes filled with woman's tears as we covered him with his blanket and left him to sleep on the field where he had fallen. Hurdle put a head and foot mark at his grave, with the inscription in pencil:

"DENNIS McDERMOTT
of the Old Dominion Rifles, of Alexandria, Va.,
died in battle
July 21, 1861
'A gallant soldier and a good man'."

Such was the story of the part taken by Alexandria's infantry in the opening battle of the War between the States. But it was not the whole story of the city's contribution to that rousing victory. Another outfit, Captain Del Kemper's Alexandria Light Artillery, had an active and noteworthy part in the fighting both on Thursday and on Sunday.

In the first clash, on the 18th, the battery was stationed at Mitchell's Ford. It was under the command of Colonel Kershaw, of the Second South Carolina, and with that regiment was thrown across the ford at one stage of the day's maneuvering to drive back a detachment of the enemy. Planting his guns on a ridge he threw his shot among the enemy with the same precision as in that first brush at Vienna, and soon brought about their discomfiture and disappearance. Our troops were then withdrawn again within our lines, having discharged the duty assigned to them.

The part which Captain Kemper's command played in the fighting on the 21st can best be told in his own words, taken from his official report:

"At 7 o'clock precisely on the morning of the 21st the enemy commenced a cannonade from his original position in front of Mitchell's Ford. My battery was ordered from the left of the trenches about 9 a. m. and placed in position in the rear of the trenches at Mitchell's Ford.

"This position was occupied without a chance to respond to the fire of the enemy, they being clearly beyond our range, until about 1 p. m., when I was ordered to join Colonels Kershaw and Cash, and under the command of Colonel Kershaw to move to the left of our lines near Stone Bridge.

"We arrived near the scene of action about 4 p. m., and immediately taking position in and near the road leading from Sudley

Ford to Manassas junction, and about one-half mile south of the turnpike, we had the honor of receiving and repulsing the last attack made by the enemy.

"They were formed in strong force (of regulars) and required to be repulsed three times before they retired finally, which they began to do about 4:15 p. m. Seeing their general retreat commenced, and my men being very much worn out, I withdrew my battery a short distance to the rear, and returning with a few of my men got one of the, Parrott rifled guns, previously captured from the enemy, in a position to bear upon their retreating column, and had the satisfaction of annoying them considerably.

"Colonel Kershaw ordered his whole command to pursue them down the turnpike and especially to endeavor to cut them off where the road from Sudley Church (by which their main body retreated) intersects the turnpike, about two and a half miles from Centreville. We failed to over take any enemy in the turnpike until we arrived on the hill, about one mile south of Cub Creek Bridge, in time to open (with two of my guns) on the enemy's column, which was by this time partly in the turnpike. We also threw, with good effect, some spherical case into their baggage train, etc., which had not emerged into the turnpike.

"I wish to remark that the first shot fired to rake the road was fired by the venerable Edmund Ruffin, and a prisoner subsequently stated that the effect was frightful. This maneuver resulted in the capture of many cannon, caissons, artillery horses, and baggage wagons, and many prisoners.

"In obedience to order, Colonel Kershaw's command returned to Stone Bridge, where we arrived about 11 p. m., and thus, as far as we were concerned, closed this glorious day.

"I desire to call attention to the gallant bearing of Lieutenants Steuart, Bayliss, and Smoot, of my company. Each of them throughout the engagements of Thursday and Sunday performed his whole duty with a degree of coolness and judgment worthy of all praise. The men of my company, with two exceptions, behaved like veterans. The casualties of my command were: One killed, Private Richard Owens, killed by a musket ball, and two wounded slightly; also one horse killed, two wounded, and one lost."

General Beauregard made special mention of Kemper's Battery in his report on the battle, and General Bonham said:

"Captain Del Kemper and the officers and men of his battery are deserving of my highest approbation. They were the first artillery to occupy Artillery Hill at Centreville under my orders. They have been kept steadily in the front, and have shown themselves worthy of the position and the great cause in which they are engaged."

Colonel J. B. Kershaw, Second Regiment South Carolina Volunteers, under whom the battery served at Manassas, also bore testimony to its efficiency.

"Captain Kemper, of the Alexandria Artillery" he said, "and all his officers and men, engaged as they were under my own eye, merit the most honorable mention in this report. To the efficiency of this battery I have no doubt we are chiefly indebted for the valuable capture of arms, stores, and munitions of war at the suspension bridge. Without this artillery they could not have been arrested."

The result of the battle on Sunday, as everyone knows, was the complete demoralization of the Union troops. Reporting to the War Department from Fairfax Court House on the day after the battle General McDowell, the Union commander, said that the men were without food, having thrown away their haversacks in the battle, and that a large part of them were a confused mob, entirely demoralized.

It was the opinion of all the commanders, he said, that no stand could be made this side of the Potomac and he was proceeding to fall back to that river. But many of the volunteers had not waited for authority to make the move and had left on their own volition. "They are now pouring through this place," he declared, "in a state of utter disorganization."

The Ellsworth Zouaves, an organization well known to the citizens of Alexandria at that time, had a conspicuous part in this famous rout. General McDowell, in the above report made on the day following the battle, said that the officer commanding the Eleventh New York Regiment (the Zouaves), reported that many of their men had gone back to New York. Colonel Andrew Porter, commanding the Second Division, 3,700 strong, of the Union Army, said: "The evanescent courage of the Zouaves prompted them to fire perhaps a hundred shots, when they broke and fled, leaving the batteries open to a charge of the enemy's cavalry." General Heintzelman reported: "Such a rout I never witnessed before; since the retreat more than one third of the Zouaves have disappeared."

On the Confederate side the result of the battle, of course, brought wild jubilation. I cannot close this brief account of Manassas better than by giving the picture of the closing hours of that day as presented by Comrade George Wise in his History of the Seventeenth Virginia Infantry:

"What a glorious day Sunday was for the South! When the rout of the enemy came down the long line of Bull Run, up went a shout! Oh, how grand it was!

"Imagine the quiet woods through which the watching bayonets glittered silently, suddenly alive with triumphant hurrahs! From right to left, and left to right, for seven miles they were repeated!

"Then came the order to advance, and as we left the woods and gained the high and open grounds, the grandest spectacle I ever saw met my eyes. Company after company, regiment after regiment, brigade after brigade, army after army of our troops appeared. We halted to enjoy the sight, and as our glorious artillery and dashing cavalry spurred by in pursuit shout after shout rent the air.

"General Longstreet, our brigade commander, rode along our line with his staff, and thousands of men flung their caps in the air or swung them on their bayonets. Colonel Corse, our gallant little colonel, got his meed of hurrahs; and an old negro who rode by with his gun got no small salute. And then the sunset came in a perfect glory of light sifted through the leaves."

CHAPTER VIII

FAIRFAX AND CENTREVILLE

ON July 23 we marched to Centreville, where we went into camp. We remained there until August 12, when we moved to Fairfax Court House, on the road leading to Alexandria, where we again went into camp. While we were at Centreville we witnessed the execution of two of the Louisiana Tigers who had been sentenced to death for insubordination.

We arrived at Fairfax during a heavy downpour of rain. Our camp ground was completely soaked, and as a result I became sick. I was immediately removed to the building of the M. E. Church, South, which had been converted into a temporary hospital, but I had been there only an hour or so when my father obtained quarters for me in the home of Mr. Whitemore. I made my bed on the floor, which to me was fine.

I had many visits from the boys, and as the parlor was nicely furnished, having among other things a grand piano, the place proved to be a great attraction for me. One of my comrades, Tip Smith, was so pleased with the surroundings that he found it necessary to obtain quarters there, much to my gratification. He was quite a musician and had a fine bass voice. While he was at this house he composed several songs, which became decidedly popular. One of them was the song called "Virginia."

I was confined to the house for about two weeks, after which I reported for duty. This was the only occasion during the entire four years when I spent a night under a roof.

Over the next six or seven months Confederate and Union forces confronted each other here in northern Virginia with out engaging in any important battle. Each side was gathering its strength for a struggle which each now recognized would be long and bitter. Camp life during this period was one of constant watchfulness, with now and then a skirmish or an exchange of shots to liven things up. There was also many a little incident, trivial in itself, which served to lighten the monotony and hardship of the camp, and which meant much to us, however unimportant it may seem to others today. Among my memories of these times many such come floating back to me.

While we were stationed here at Fairfax Court House one member of our regiment who occasionally imbibed too much had leave of absence to visit the village. While there he became intoxicated and presently was taken care of and, by order of the provost marshal, locked up in the court house building, the second floor of which was used as a guardhouse.

He found there a good many other prisoners confined on the same charge. One of them was a member of the famous Louisiana Tigers. Our own man was going about the room, bellowing in imitation of a bull and calling out, "I'm a bull! I'm a bull!" when the Louisiana man rushed upon him with the shout, "I'm a tiger!" and roaring like one grabbed the Seventeenth around the waist, pulled him to the window, and pitched him clear out to the ground below, breaking his leg.

It is but just to our comrade to state that he ranked as one of the best soldiers in the regiment - in fact, it stands to his credit that he never missed a fight in which his regiment was engaged. He survived the war and died at his home in Alexandria.

Here at Fairfax our time was occupied in performing ordinary camp duties and in picketing the country below, in the neighborhood of Falls Church, Upton and Munson's Hills. A day or two after I had reported for duty my company was sent to Falls Church, where it was stationed for a few days.

One night while we were quietly resting it was thought necessary, for some reason or other to strengthen the pickets on the outposts. I was called up with a number of others at about 10 o'clock to go on that duty. It was dark and raining. I was posted at a fence with Comrade Bud Baldwin, of Company H. The night passed quietly, except for a slight alarm just before daylight which amounted to nothing, but we were very much amused in the morning listening to the roll call of the company of the enemy in front of us as it was called off by the sergeant. It was evidently a Maryland regiment, as it had quite a number of men whose names were similar to mine. As each of these names was called it was promptly answered "Here!" from our side.

We felt it almost our bounded duty to have a little fight every day at the Peach Orchard on Munson's Hill. While I was on picket here one day, with the enemy in possession of the orchard, a Yankee climbed up on a gate post and began cutting up, going through such antics as twirling his fingers on his nose, shaking his fists, and dancing.

We had with us it this time a volunteer scout from Texas by the name of Fort. He was a fine shot, and it was decided to call him to the front and give him a chance at the fellow on the post. Fort crawled up on him as close as he thought necessary, sighted his Sharpe's rifle for a long-distance shot, and fired. The man fell, and it was some time before any of his comrades ventured to come out and get his body for fear the same marksman was waiting for them.

On another occasion the boys mounted a section of an old stovepipe on two wheels which they had obtained at a wheelwright shop at the crossroads. It was a favorite trick to run it out into the center of the road and go through the motions of loading a gun and pointing it at the enemy, who promptly stampeded, under the impression that we had a piece of artillery with us. General Longstreet in his history makes mention of this incident.

One night when we were occupying an old schoolhouse as quarters for the reserve pickets the lights were ordered out. Then the storm began. The mischievous ones among us commenced throwing shoes, cartridge boxes, haversacks, and anything else they could find within reach about the room and mixing things up generally in the dark. Then suddenly the pickets outside began firing briskly, the sentinel at the door gave the alarm, the order came to fall in, and what a predicament the company was in! Many of the boys fell in line without shoes, some had belts and cartridge boxes that belonged to others, and confusion reigned supreme. Fortunately our pickets drove back those of the enemy. Order was restored, lights procured, and things put to right, but the incident taught the boys a lesson they never forgot.

About this time our company lost a splendid officer, Lieutenant Douglass F. Forrest. He received an appointment on the staff of General Trimble, who was then stationed at Evansport on the Potomac River.

Our regiment at this time had present for duty 665 men, and 80 unfit for duty, making a total in camp of 745. Those absent on detailed service numbered 33; absent with leave, 4; absent without leave, 11;

absent sick and wounded, 101; making a total of men absent of 149. The total number on the roll of officers and men was thus 894.

While we were stationed here we were frequently called out to go to the front to meet the enemy, but for the most part these alarms proved to be nothing more than opportune ties for good exercise for the men. During the night of August 31, while we were doing picket duty at Mason's and Munson's Hills, we were relieved by two regiments of Early's brigade, the Twenty-fourth Virginia and Fifth North Carolina. They found us on the outpost about one mile from the main line in the direction of Alexandria. From this position we were in full view of the Capitol building at Washington and also of the camps of the enemy, west of Alexandria.

We were constantly skirmishing with the Union pickets. Once we had quite a brisk fight with the Third New Jersey Regiment, which we repulsed with some little loss to them. After this fight they sent over a flag of truce for the purpose of getting their dead. This duty was attended to by General Early's command, which was stationed at Fairfax Station.

On October 3 the army was reviewed by President Davis. About the middle of that month we lost our brigade commander, General Longstreet. He was promoted to the command of a division, with the rank of major general. The following was read to the regiments of the brigade:

"Headquarters Fourth Brigade,
First Corps,
A. P. Fairfax C. H., October 13, 1861.
"General Order No. 17"

"In relinquishing the command of the Fourth Brigade, First Corps, Army of the Potomac, the Commanding General expresses his sincere thanks to the officers and soldiers of the command for the kindly patience, the soldierly fortitude, and the cheerful obedience which they have invariably exhibited during the many hardships and privations of a long and trying campaign.

"The command of a brigade second to none is well worthy the boast of any general, and even regret may well be felt at promotion which removes it a step, at least, from him.

"By command of Maj.-Gen. Longstreet.

"G. Moxley Sorrel,
"Capt. and A. A. G."

General Longstreet was succeeded by General Clark, of Mississippi, who was transferred after a few days to another brigade connected with the Army of the West, and on the 8th General Richard S. Ewell became our commander. At this time the Seventh Virginia Regiment was added to our brigade.

While we were here our boys played a trick on the colonel. It seems that it had become noised about in the camps of the other troops that liquor could be had over in the camp of the Seventeenth Virginia. Now it is well known that having whiskey in camp is a gross violation of military discipline and order, and when any is passed around at all it must be very quietly and on the sly. The little incident I mention came about in this manner:

A long, lank North Carolinian presented himself among our boys, searching quietly for the fellow who had the juice for sale. With a great deal of apparent caution he was called aside and told where he could obtain the desired article. He was informed that an officer was the only one who had any left, and that the officer was very cautious and particular as to whom he sold. The colonel's tent was pointed out to him as the place to apply. The boys told him further that the officer was suspicious of strangers and might not want to let him have it, but that by persisting he would be sure to get it.

To the colonel's tent he went, and the scene that followed can be imagined. The colonel was, of course, taken by surprise by his customer, and when he told the rascal to get out or he would have him put out, the soldier replied:

"Oh, I know you have got the whiskey, but you are too proud to sell it to a private."

The poor fellow had finally to be put out of camp, much to the amusement of the boys, who had been listening to the whole proceeding.

Also at this camp the boys arranged dress parades as burlesque imitations of the regular dress parades held every afternoon while we were in camp. On these occasions all the real parades would be observed, with the men dressing and arming themselves in the most ludicrous manner. The bogus adjutant would read out the orders, which were usually of a comic nature, burlesquing those which had previously been read by the regular adjutant. The band would consist of ten to twenty men under a comically arrayed drum major, who performed the usual antics of that functionary. The music was produced by playing on combs covered with paper and was accompanied by the beating of drums to all sorts of time. Altogether the show was quite an entertaining one for the numerous visitors who came from the other camps to see it.

On the night of October 16 orders came to vacate our camp and retire to Centreville. It was with real regret that we left Fairfax. We had spent many pleasant hours at the place, and it was so near home for many of us. But such is the soldier's lot. Previous to leaving camp details were named from several regiments to move the telegraph wires and take them to Centreville. The next morning found us pitching our tents on our new camp grounds on the heights near the village of Centreville, where we were destined to remain until early in March, 1862.

During these winter months our time was fully taken up with drilling, mounting Quaker guns, standing picket duty, and doing our part in the details set to the work of throwing up breastworks.

While we were here the state, through its governor, the Hon. John Letcher, presented us with the flag of Virginia. (It is now in the possession of the R. E. Lee camp of this city.) This flag was superseded on November 28 by the flag adopted by the Confederate States authorities and known as the "battle-flag". After the Battles of Bull Run and Manassas and before the adoption of the battleflag the Confederate Government requested that each state should furnish to its regiments its own state flag, but Virginia was the only one that had complied with the request.

While the ceremony of presentation of the Virginia flag was going on the enemy sent up a captive balloon from Hall's Hill, which hovered over us. The governor, looking up, said: "I reckon that fellow up there thinks its h--- to pay down here."

On the night of November 1 we experienced one of the most terrific storms of wind, rain, and hail that we had to contend with during the war. The storm continued throughout the night. Every tent in the camp except two was thrown down and the contents were scattered. The storm did not cease until the afternoon of the 2nd, and during that time the men were without shelter, thoroughly drenched, and unable to cook their meals.

An incident of which I happened to be the central figure and which furnished plenty of amusement to the other boys but not so much to me at the time occured while we were in camp here.

For a while we had our station for picket duty at Germantown, about one and one-half miles west of Fairfax Court House. Company D, which hailed from Fairfax, was doing picket duty at this post when Colonel Corse of our regiment received a message by courier from Colonel J. E. B. Stuart, who commanded the outpost, inquiring the name of the officer who had just gone through the lines in the direction of the village accompanied by a lady.

Inquiry was made, and the officer in question was found to be Captain Rosser, then in command of a company of the Washington Artillery, which was also on picket duty. The lady was a prominent resident of the village whom the captain had been escorting to her home. He had returned in the meantime. On learning this Colonel Stuart sent word to our colonel to place Captain Rosser under arrest, and the order was entrusted to me to carry to the captain.

I was starting out on foot to do so when the colonel insisted on my riding one of his horses. He had two, ready saddled and bridled, called "Bayonet" and "Bullet". "Bullet" was the one selected for me. Not being much of a rider at best I had my doubts about being able to mount and manage him, especially as I had seen him unseat the Colonel a few days before while the officer was drilling the regiment. But I tried it, nevertheless, and succeeding in getting on I started to find the Captain. He was with his battery, which was parked in a field less than a mile in the rear of our line.

My horse promptly ran away with me, and between my fright at not being able to check him and my efforts to retain my seat in the saddle I found it impossible to give the signal required at the inner light of pickets. But the guards recognized me, and seeing the predicament I was in merely cheered me on as I passed on my journey.

I was soon in sight of Rosser's camp. Most of the men were amusing themselves sailing small toy boats in a nearby pond. Seeing a rapidly approaching horseman coming from the front they naturally supposed him to be a courier sent for them. They immediately quit their pastime and rushed to their horses, and by the time I reached the opening to their camp they were ready to mount at the order.

I managed somehow to turn my horse into the field, and rode for the quarters. Noticing the commotion among his men Rosser came out, and I got my horse stopped and delivered the order to him. He read it, turned the command over to his lieutenant, and waved to his men to unhitch. So far as they were concerned the incident was closed. But it was a long time before I heard the last of my ride from the boys in the camp.

On returning I was careful not to let my horse get out of a walk. I did not want him to take me into the line of the enemy, and he was headed in that direction. Captain Rosser's career, incidentally, apparently received no injury from his arrest. On June 10, 1862, he was promoted on the field for gallantry to the rank of lieutenant colonel of artillery, and on the 20th of the same month he was made colonel of cavalry and assigned to the command of the Fifth Virginia Regiment.

On November 8 Company H, the Old Dominion Rifles, voted to enlist for two years more, thus making its total enlistment three years. Its example was followed by the other companies of the regiment.

On November 28, 1861, the new battle-flag, as mentioned above, made its appearance. The following order was read to the troops:

"A new banner is intrusted today, as a battle-flag, to the safekeeping of the army of the Potomac.

"Soldiers, your mothers, your wives, and your sisters made it. It must lead you to substantial victory and the complete triumph of our cause.

"It can never be surrendered, save to your unspeakable dishonor and with consequence fraught with immeasurable evil.

"Under its untarnished folds, beat back the invader and find nationality, everlasting immunity from an atrocious despotism, and honor and renown for yourselves, or death.

"By command of General Beauregard.

"Thomas Jordan, A. A. General."

On November 30 a grand review of Longstreet's Division took place. It passed off to the satisfaction of the general and the troops. On December 5 General Beauregard from headquarters at Centreville sent to General Longstreet an order to prepare what were known with us as Quaker guns, to be placed in our batteries on the heights at Centreville to deceive the enemy. They consisted of pieces of wood of the proper size, blackened to represent guns. They were partially protected from the view of the enemy lookouts in the balloons which occasionally hovered over our camps by rough sheds covered with leaves and brushwood.

On December 20 the Eleventh Regiment, of our brigade, while out with a foraging party, was attacked by the enemy and lost about fifty men, killed, wounded, and missing. When the bodies of the dead were brought in for burial our regiment attended the interment in a body, prompted by the friendly feeling that had existed between the two commands ever since the organization of the brigade. The act brought forth from Colonel Garland of the Eleventh a beautiful letter, which was read on dress parade, expressing his grateful appreciation of the soldierly friendship which induced our command to unite with them in paying this last tribute of respect to their dead comrades.

While we were here at camp our army was reviewed by Prince Napoleon, who came through the lines after visiting and reviewing the Union army.

Our first Christmas found us here at Centreville, with the ground covered with snow and the weather bitter cold. Many of the boys from the other companies of our regiment whose homes were not within the lines of the enemy received presents from home, but none came to the Alexandria exiles.

On January 29 General Beauregard asked for the appointment of Major George Williams Brent as inspector general, and that of Captain S. W. Prestman as topographical engineer. Both were members of the Seventeenth Virginia and the regiment regretted losing these two valuable officers.

CHAPTER IX

FIRST DEFENSE OF RICHMOND

WE passed the winter, with all its hardships and sufferings, as became men who had voluntarily made this sacrifice for our common cause. Inactivity ended on March 9, 1862, when we evacuated Centreville, marching through Warrenton towards Culpeper.

Notwithstanding the fact that our evacuation was voluntary, in the sense that it was not forced by the enemy, we burned large quantities of stores by order of General Johnston. Our regiment, although it could ill afford the loss, had to give up much of its baggage. We also left here at Centreville as a legacy to our friends, the enemy, all our dummy wooden cannon which were mounted in our forts and redoubts, and in order to deceive and delay the enemy we manned the forts and batteries with dummy soldiers.

While on this march we learned of the glorious victory of our ironclad *Virginia* over the United States fleet at Hampton Roads, which occurred March 8, 1862. Our command finally reached the neighborhood of Orange Court House on March 17 and went into camp, remaining there until April 6.

At this time we lost by promotion our brigade commander, General Richard S. Ewell. Colonel A. P. Hill of the Thirteenth Virginia was assigned to the command. At the time this assignment was not popular with many of our regiment, they preferring the appointment of our colonel, M. D. Corse. But a month later when General Hill, with the colors of our regiment, led the fight at Williamsburg, he became the idol of his troops. At this time we also bade farewell to Major George William Brent, who left us for his assignment to duty as inspector general of the Army of the West, commanded by General Beauregard. He was afterwards promoted and assigned to duty as adjutant general, serving under Generals Bragg and Johnston until the close of the war. On April 15, 1862, Colonel Julius A. de Lagnel of Alexandria was appointed brigadier general, but he declined the appointment.

After leaving the camp near Orange Court House we bivouacked near Louisa Court House for two days, and then continued our march to Richmond. We marched through that city and were put on a steamboat at Rocket's. Passing down the river through the obstructions at Drewry's Bluff we landed at King's Mill Wharf, and after a hurried march went into the trenches near Yorktown, occupying a position near Dam No. 1. We reached there on April 17. General Magruder was in command of the Confederate forces at this point until the arrival of the army under General Johnston, when the latter assumed command.

Magruder's line was about thirteen miles in length, running along Warwick River. The river was really little more than a succession of marshes. About a mile and a half to the right of Yorktown was a sluggish stream, running through dense woods and many swamps.

Along the river were two main dams, one at Wynne's Mill and the other at Lee's Mill, and three others were constructed along the line. These dams raised the water of the stream so high that for most of its course it was impracticable for either infantry or artillery to cross. The dams were designated by numbers.

We were kept here about two weeks, suffering severely from the continued sniping of the Union sharpshooters. We lost three good men in one day through these sharpshooters - Lyman Coons, of Company D, and Henry Biggs and A. F. Skidmore, both of Company E. The two last-named were hit by the same bullet, which was fired from a tree just in front of our position. It passed through Biggs' neck and entered Skidmore's stomach, killing him instantly.

In spite of such sniping, and notwithstanding the disposition of the opposing forces to fire on each other at the slightest manifestation of an advance or a desire to gain advantages, there was much kindly feeling at times among the men of each army for those of the other and when opportunities offered it would frequently show itself.

There was a good deal of trading of coffee, newspapers, tobacco, and other things. I remember well that once while we were lying in the trenches near Yorktown a poor old dog in some way found himself between the lines. We whistled to him and coaxed him into our lines. Some enterprising individual securely tied some tobacco about his neck, and he was put outside our works and driven over to the enemy, who in turn were whistling for him. Having received the tobacco, they tied a small bag of coffee in its place and the dog was sent on his return trip. Several exchanges were made in this manner until orders put a stop to the traffic.

One day, near Dam No. 1, I was looking on while four of the boys of Company H were playing a game of cards. They were lying under a small tent fly, with their heads' together. In the center of the group, on the ground, they had placed an inverted tin cup and had put on it some grains of corn to represent the money for which they were playing. A shell burst directed, over our heads, scattering pieces all around, and one small piece came through the canvas and stuck in the bottom of the cup. It did not disturb the game, which continued steadily on. I fell heir to the cup and sent it on to Richmond for safe keeping. And that was the last I ever saw of it.

Under an act of Congress we were allowed to reorganize our regiments, and we did so while here. In an election of officers held on April 26 Colonel M. D. Corse was re-elected, Captain Morton Marye of Company A was made lieutenant colonel, and Captain Arthur Herbert of Company H was made major. Changes were made in all the companies of the regiment. Lieutenant William H. Fowle was promoted to the captaincy of Company H, Lieutenant A. J. Humphries became captain of Company A, and Lieutenant NV. B. Lynch captain of Company C. Captains of other companies were chosen as follows: Company D, Lieutenant J. T. Burke; Company E, Lieutenant James M. Steuart; Company F, Lieutenant Grayson Tyler; Company G, Lieutenant Robert F. Knox; Company I, Lieutenant Raymond Fairfax; Company K, Lieutenant J. D. Kirby.

We left the trenches at this place on the night of Saturday, May 3, and never were orders more gladly received than those that took us away. Most of the time while here we were sleeping on damp and soggy ground, as it rained almost continually. We arrived at Williamsburg the next day, May 4, after marching over roads that were in a horrible condition on account of the rains, and were placed in line of battle for the fight of the following day.

The Battle of Williamsburg, fought on the 5th of May, was stubbornly contested. It lasted the entire day, in an almost continuous rain and resulted in our driving the enemy back, our forces gaining ground and checking the Union advance.

In this severe fighting our brigade had its full share and our losses were heavy. As to the conduct of men and officers the laudatory words of the commanding officers are sufficient testimony that they acquitted themselves with all honor.

"It was long and hotly engaged," says General Longstreet, referring to our brigade (A. P. Hill's). "Ably led by its commanders, it drove the enemy from every position. This brigade, composed of the First, Seventh, Eleventh, and Seventeenth Virginia Infantry, from its severe loss must have been in the thickest of the fight. Its organization was perfect throughout the battle, and it was marched off the field in as good order as when it entered."

Our own commander, General A. P. Hill, says: "My own was actively and constantly engaged in the front for seven hours. Many of our men fired over sixty rounds of cartridges, and for two hours longer we were lying passive under a heavy fire, ready to spring to it again should the enemy rally to the fight.

"We drove the enemy from every position he took, captured all his knapsacks, and never suffered him to regain an inch of lost ground. My own brigade was fortunate in taking seven stands of colors and about 160 prisoners, and shared with the Ninth Alabama the honor of taking eight pieces of artillery."

General J. E. B. Stuart, commander of our cavalry, who was on this field, speaks in the highest terms of the heroic courage and fighting tact of the Eleventh and Seventeenth Virginia of Hill's brigade.

In this fight our regiment captured two flags and quite a number of band instruments. The boys left the field blowing the horns and beating the drums.

There was jubilation over our successful stand at Williamsburg, but there was also grief at the heavy cost. Our regiment paid its full share of the cost. Among the places used as a hospital was the old historic Bruton Parish Church, where we were compelled to leave a number of our seriously wounded. I recollect that among them were Captain A. J. Humphries, of Company A; noncommissioned officers E. P. Barbour and James E. Grimes, of Company 11; and Privates Clinton Ballenger and Pat Lannon, also of Company, H. All died during the night. There were a number of other deaths and many wounded, both officers and privates.***

That night and the morning after the fight we continued our march to Richmond. It was a march long to be remembered. To quote the words of General E. P. Alexander: "The sufferings of that night will probably never be forgotten, either by the wornout brigade who, after the long day's fight, waded and stumbled all night in the mud; or by those who, without fires, crouched along the lines until near lay light, and then set forth again on the march; or by the wounded, who lay on the field until found by the enemy next day, as many unfortunately did."

On this march I recall that I was detailed with a number of others at midnight to assist in pulling out of the mud a battery that was mired down. Horses were brought back from the guns that had succeeded in getting through and were hitched on, while we pulled at the ropes, wading knee deep in the mud. In this manner, working by the light of torches and bonfires, we managed to get the guns out.

We passed through Richmond and as a compliment to the regiment we were allowed to carry the captured Stars and Stripes at its head. We went into camp at Christian's Farm and remained there a few days resting. Then we moved to Deep Bottom on the James River, where we did picket duty for several days. While here our skirmishers had an encounter with a gunboat in which we had one man wounded. Our next move carried us from Deep bottom nearer to Richmond, where we again went into camp to await the next move of the commanders.

General McClellan, in command of the Union army, was placing his forces in position for an attempt to capture Richmond, while the Confederates were busy recruiting their army and strengthening the defenses of their capital city.

We passed our time in front of the city in doing guard duty and individual blockade running into the city. And many were the devices resorted to by which to accomplish the latter feat.

We had in our company a man by the name of Smith who could imitate so successfully the signature of Colonel Corse that the colonel

---

*** A partial list of the casualties in the different companies of the regiment will be found in the Appendix.

71

himself had to acknowledge that he could not tell the difference. Many of the boys made trips to Richmond on passes signed by Smith. But that was too good to last. The discovery that bogus passes were being used came about when Army headquarters, anticipating trouble on the front, issued orders that positively no passes should be granted on the next day and everyone should be held in the line. The boys did not know about this order and the usual custom prevailed. When the guards were posted they received orders not to recognize any passes. Notwithstanding, a pass claiming to come from our colonel was tendered the guard, who reported the fact. Then followed an investigation as to who had issued that pass. The colonel admitted that but for the fact that he had not signed a single pass that day he would have had to admit that the signature so perfectly written was his own. When the writer was discovered nothing was done.

One day when I was on my way to the city with a pass I met three others of my company who did not have passes. Their whole thought was how to get into the city without being caught. After a short consultation it was decided that I should assume the role of a prisoner under guard, and as such they would carry me through the line into the city.

Approaching the picket, who was posted at the Manchester side of the Mayo Bridge, which spanned the James River at that point, we were duly halted and the sergeant stated that he and his guard had a prisoner, with orders to take him to the Soldiers' Home on Cary Street. After some little parleying the picket allowed the guard to pass with the prisoner. I remained a prisoner until we were out of sight of the picket, when we separated and each one was free to go where he pleased.

CHAPTER X

HARD FIGHTING AROUND RICHMOND

THUS time passed until the latter part of the month, when again the troops were called upon to do battle and make an effort to drive the enemy from around Richmond.

Friday night, May 30, 1862, found me with a number of my comrades in the city, where we had gone to attend a minstrel performance of "White's Iron-Clad Minstrels" at the theater near the Ballard Hotel on Franklin Street. Charles 0. White, the proprietor and manager, was an Alexandrian. At that same time, at the Richmond Theater on Broad Street (which was under the management of Mrs. McGill), Miss Katie Estelle, a great favorite with the Alexandria public previous to the commencement of hostilities, was playing the leading part in "Lucretia Borgia" with R. D'Osay Ogden in the role of Genaro.

We returned to the camp at midnight in the midst of a terrible storm of wind, rain, and vivid lightning and found it deluged and in impenetrable darkness except for the occasional lightning flashes. In his history "From Manassas to Appomattox" Longstreet after the war described this storm: "A terrific storm of vivid lightning, thunderbolts, and rain, as severe as ever known to any climate, burst upon us and continued through the night more or less severe." And a northern writer even more graphically wrote of it: "That night the 'windows of heaven seemed to have been opened' and the 'fountains of the deep broken up.' The storm fell like a deluge. It was the most violent storm that had swept over that region for a generation. Through out the night the tempest raged. The thunderbolts rolled without cessation. The sky was white with the electric flashes. The earth was thoroughly drenched. The low lands became a morass. From mud-soaked beds the soldiers arose the next morning to battle."

Shortly after the rain ceased we were disturbed by a courier. The delivery of his message was followed by the long roll. Rations were ordered for two days, and at dawn we fell into line and marched to our position, ready to take part in the great Battle of Seven Pines, or as the enemy called it, the "Battle of Fair Oaks." Our position at first was in the rear, as the reserve.

The battle began about 1 o'clock and raged all afternoon. At about 4 o'clock it was our turn to go to the front, which we did at a double quick, charging the enemy and driving them through their camps. Our regiment was relieved at about 9 o'clock that night and ordered to the rear.

In this fight the casualties were again heavy, both for the army and for our own regiment and company. General Joseph E. Johnston, our commander, was severely wounded. He was succeeded by General Gustavus W. Smith, who was relieved the next day by General Robert E. Lee.

My company, the Old Dominion Rifles, carried in about fifty boys. Of that number eighteen were killed or wounded. One of those killed was Rodie Whittington, a classmate of mine. He had just joined our company the evening before and had answered only one roll call. He was buried with his companions, Higdon, Lunt, and Murray, within the fort captured from the enemy. They were simply wrapped in their blankets.

The loss to the regiment was seventy-four killed and wounded.**** Among the casualties were Sergeant Major J. F. Francis, who was killed, and Major Arthur Herbert, who was wounded. Major Herbert received his wound while crossing the battle front to take command of an Alabama regiment that had lost all its officers, he having volunteered for that duty.

Sergeant Morrill, color-bearer of the regiment, was killed while carrying the colors. Captain Raymond Fairfax, of Company 1, caught up the colors and turned them over to Corporal Diggs, of Company E, who fell severely wounded. Private Washington M. Harper then bore the flag in safety until the end of the battle. Harper was a gallant soldier and was killed at the Battle of Sharpsburg, in Maryland, on September 17, while carrying the colors of the regiment.

Among the little incidents at this Battle of Seven Pines which have remained in my memory is one which occurred while we were lying in reserve.

**** See Appendix.

74

A young soldier from the front came running up the road, almost out of breath. Major Herbert stepped out into the road and held him up. He proved to be a very much demoralized young person, and on being questioned he told of how his regiment was almost entirely annihilated. Only he and a few others were left.

The major told him to stay with us and rest himself. He told his name and the command to which he belonged and we found afterwards that his regiment had been severely handled by the enemy. The major put him in Company A, telling him to report after the fight to him. When the fight was over the major gave him a fine letter to take back to his colonel, stating how the young soldier had been found after becoming separated from his command and how he had joined our regiment and gone into the fight with it, and adding that he had behaved splendidly. The boy was quite proud of this letter, and left us to rejoin his comrades.

Comrade George Wise, of Company H, in his history of the Seventeenth Virginia Regiment, relates the following true incident of the Battle of Seven Pines:

"During the battle in the redoubt James H. Watkins, of Company H, and Alexander Hunter, of Company A, were particularly conspicuous in the heat of the first day's fight for bravery and unerring aim. Guns were loaded by the boys around them and the two, standing upon the embankment, fired as rapidly as they could take the guns. The colors of a regiment in front of us were cut down three times in succession."

The foe that our brigade met face to face was the brigade of General Nagles, and our immediate opponents were the Fifty-sixth and Eleventh Maine.

On June 1 the army, which up to this time had borne the name "Army of the Potomac," was rechristened "Army of Northern Virginia." Our regiment on Monday returned to its camp, where we remained until June 26, when we were ordered again to prepare to march. Several day's rations were cooked and we moved in the direction of Mechanicsville, where we slept on the pike. Here the battle order of General Longstreet was read to us. I can recall only the last lines, which were, "Aim low, and keep cool, and your general will be responsible for the issue."

During the night of Thursday, the 26th, an amusing incident occurred. While we were sleeping a number of artillery horses broke loose and galloped down the road on which we lay. With their rattling traces they sounded like troop of cavalry, and the cry was raised that the Yankee cavalry was upon us. Many of the men, still half-dazed with sleep, jumped into a ditch by the roadside and were thoroughly drenched and covered with mud. Our colonel was one of them. I did not jump, and thereby saved myself a wetting. Order was soon restored and we quietly turned in for another nap, to be prepared for the expected hard work of the morrow.

At about 4 o'clock in the morning of Friday, the 27th, we crossed the Chickahominy and moved forward in the direction of the fight then in progress. This fight was brought on by a spirited attack made by General A. P. Hill on the Federal force at Mechanicsville at that hour, he having received information that Jackson had arrived from the Valley.

We were so close upon the enemy, who were directly in our front and who began to fall back as we advanced, that they had time to destroy but little of their commissary and quartermaster stores. Our regiment was halted for a few moments near the blazing stores, and it fell to my lot to become the owner of a large quantity of ground coffee, which I was able to save by dividing with one of the wagon drivers of our brigade. I also managed to get some salt pork but the commissary of the regiment took it away from us that night when we went into camp.

While we were pushing forward after the retreating enemy the Otey battery of Lynchburg passed us galloping to the front. Several Alexandrians were in this battery. One of them, James H. Reid, a former schoolmate of mine, called out to me as they passed.

This fight was the beginning of the "Seven Days" fighting around Richmond. Jackson had come down from the Valley with his victorious troops and was now thundering in the rear of the enemy's right. The fact gave renewed vigor to the main army and all moved forward, confident of final victory. Two days had now passed and both were glorious days to the Confederates.

76

My company, with one other of the regiment, was detailed to guard nearly 1,500 prisoners on their way to Richmond. But we returned to the regiment the next day, having been relieved by some local troops before reaching the city.

The fight on Saturday, the 28th, as on the two previous days was favorable to the Confederates, the enemy being constantly pushed back. On Sunday we crossed the Chickahominy on the "Grape-vine" bridge. Up to this time we had been held in reserve in close call to the battle front, moving along just in the rear of the front line and keeping up with it. The enemy had now reached Frazier's Farm and on Monday, June 30, our brigade under the command of General James L. Kemper was formed in line of battle. It's time had come for work.

The day set in extremely warm, as several preceding days had been. In forming, our regiment was on the right of the brigade and the brigade was on the right of the line of the division, which was under the command of General R. H. Anderson , our regular division commander. The formation was complete and everything was in readiness for an attack by 2 o'clock p. m. But General Lee, who was on the field with President Davis, directed that it should be delayed until Jackson or Huger should be heard from. This delay held us up and it was about 4 o'clock in the afternoon when we were ordered to advance upon the enemy. In doing so we had to march several hundred yards before reaching the high ground on which their batteries were placed, passing over much broken ground and through a swamp difficult to penetrate on account of entangled vines.

General E. P. Alexander, chief of artillery of Longstreet's Corps, who was present, thus describes this advance:

"The order to move forward and attack was first received by Kemper's brigade, which held the right flank in the dense wood, with its right regiment (the Seventeenth Virginia) thrown back to protect the flank. In hearing of the order to charge, through some misapprehension the brigade started before General Kemper was able to wheel the Seventeenth into line with the others, and as it was impossible to control promptly so extensive a line in such tangled undergrowth the remaining regiments were allowed to move on, and this one, the Seventeenth, was directed to follow as soon as it could change its front.

"After advancing several hundred yards in good order in spite of swamp ground and a sharp shelling of the woods by the enemy, the Yankee pickets were discovered retiring, on seeing which the line immediately cheered loudly and took the double quick in pursuit.

"This pace soon brought them to the open field, across which were seen the Federal infantry and batteries. A terrible fire was now poured upon them but without halting to reform the line, disintegrated and much reduced by the double quick through the woods, a charge was made upon a battery (Kern's) about three hundred yards distant, supported by Seymour's brigade, the left brigade of McCall's division.

"The impetuosity of the charge broke the enemy's line and for a time the battery was in our possession. But the handful of men who gained it were unable to maintain it long, before the heavy attacks in front and flank which fell upon them as soon as their small force was appreciated, and they were soon compelled to retreat. The Seventeenth Virginia, following in rear of the rest of the brigade, had also become much scattered in its rapid movements in the forest but considerable portions of it came out in time to assist in covering the retreat of their comrades, whom the enemy pursued back into the woods.

"Meanwhile, about the time that our brigade had penetrated the enemy's line Pickett's brigade of A. P. Hill's division was hurried forward to its support and succeeded in checking the enemy and, making a gallant charge, captured the guns of the battery, turning them upon the enemy and completely routing Seymour's brigade."

The casualties of our regiment in this battle were 18 killed and 23 wounded.***** In addition 73 were taken prisoner, making the total loss 114. After the fight the usual details were made for bringing in the wounded, burying the dead, and assisting the surgeons at the field hospital. This hospital was located behind several large stacks of hay on the battlefield, just in rear of where our regiment fought. While I was helping out with the wounded an incident occurred which I will relate.

I had been assigned to look after the slightly wounded. I came upon a Union soldier with a scalp wound and while I was dressing it my attention was attracted to the cap he had with him. I recognized it by

---

***** See Appendix.

the name cut on the visor as the property of my brother. I asked him how he came in possession of it and he answered that he had lost his own and had taken this one from a dead Confederate soldier lying near him. I questioned him closely as to whether the owner was really dead but he was positive, saying that they had both fallen within arm's reach of each other.

This was the first information I had of my brother's death. Although he had been missing, I had been buoyed up with the hope that he might have been numbered among the prisoners captured by the enemy. When we had started on this charge he was about thirty yards on my right, in line, and was fighting in his shirt sleeves. As I afterward learned, he fell, shot through the breast, and was bayonetted in the stomach after he fell. He was killed at the most advanced point reached by our regiment.

I hurried through my work on the prisoner and started in search of my brother's body, hoping to find it before the darkness came. It was then about sundown. After wandering over the field, strewn with hundreds of dead and dying of both armies, I failed to find it but I finally came up with the burial detail. With the aid of torches of burning wood they had just finished their work of burying all of the regiment's dead that they could find, and were returning. Our surgeon, Dr. Harold Snowden, who was in charge of the detail, then told me that he had just finished burying my brother. He was buried with three others of the regiment, all in one shallow grave, near where he fell. The others were Daniel Lee and Conrad Johnson of Company A and Hayden Fewell of Company H.

On the following morning, Tuesday, I figured in another little event connected with this fight which led to the report that I had been wounded. My companion in it was Sergeant J. P. Jordan of my company, who afterwards published a story of it.

As Jordan tells in his story, he had been badly wounded. He had been shot twice in the foot and had also been struck by a ball in the shoulder, which had knocked him down and broken his collarbone. He was taken prisoner and sent to the rear, where he was placed with a large number of Union wounded, in due time receiving attention from a Federal surgeon.

General Fitz John Porter, who had learned that there was a Confederate prisoner among their wounded, came over and questioned him in regard to our forces. One of the questions asked was whether Longstreet had been engaged in any of the battles of the last five days, or was he, Porter, engaged with fresh Confederate troops. Jordan told him that we were entirely fresh, having been in none of the previous battles, but that he would not answer any more questions.

A little later on a Federal soldier employed as a nurse came over to him and said that he had just overheard General Porter tell the surgeons in charge of the field hospital to send all the slightly wounded to the rear, as they would begin retiring at 12 o'clock that night and would leave the badly wounded on the field. Jordan asked the nurse to place him among the latter so that he would not be carried off with the slightly wounded, and this was done. The nurse further said that he was tired of the war and that, if protected, he would remain behind and let himself fall into the hands of the Confederates. Jordan agreed to see that he had the necessary protection if the nurse would bring him a canteen of water, which he did.

From his position, Jordan writes, he could see the country road just a little distance off. About daybreak, the next morning he saw Confederate troops passing rapidly along the road following up the Federals.

"There was a rush of gray coats by the place where I was lying," he continues. "I saw comrade Ed. Warfield of my company. I called to him and he came over and lay down by the side of me and expressed surprise at finding me among the Federal wounded.

"After a short talk Warfield said, 'I must get you out of this.' With his assistance I managed to reach our lines, where we found that the good people of Richmond had brought out to the field every piece of conveyance that could be had to carry back to the city all who were wounded. My comrade saw me comfortably fixed in one and then left to rejoin his command, and in a few hours I reached Richmond."

My father, who was attached to Stonewall Jackson's command, had heard a rumor that my brother was killed and that I had been wounded and carried to a Richmond hospital. He made a search throughout the various hospitals and when he failed to find me he

80

started to find the regiment, when he learned the true condition of affairs.

Before leaving the battlefield, in company and with the assistance of a comrade, James H. Reid, of the Otey battery, who had come over from his command to learn how the Seventeenth Virginia had fared in this battle, I marked my brother's grave, giving his name, regiment, and home. This I did on a barrel stave which we found on the field nearby. Passing the spot two years later I renewed the mining and this enabled me to identify the grave after the close of the war. His body was brought home to Alexandria and buried on Thanksgiving Day, November, 1865.

The foe in our immediate front in this battle consisted of the Sixteenth Massachusetts and the Second New York Regiments. A Union writer, referring to the Battle of Frazier's Farm, says:

"On the 30th June occurred that terrible action at Frazier's Farm. The battle-line extended from White Oak Swamp through Glendale to Malvern Hill, a deployment seven miles long. The fighting qualities of these troops were so superior that they took batteries in hand-to-hand combat without the aid of a single gun. When this terrible onslaught terminated with the night McClellan succeeded in withdrawing."

CHAPTER XI

A WAR STORY

WE remained camped about six miles below Richmond until August 10, when we moved at daylight into Richmond. We took the train for Gordonsville, reaching there that night. After remaining there several days we were ordered in the direction of Orange Court House, then on to Kelley's Ford, on the Rappahannock River. There we had a little shelling from a Union battery on the opposite bank, but one of our batteries (Rogers' Loudoun) succeeded in driving it off.

We then took up our march with the rest of Longstreet's corps on the route to the support of Jackson, who was on the way to capture Manassas in the rear of Pope's army. He succeeded in doing so but in turn was compelled to defend himself against the entire Union army until relief came from Longstreet. The situation and condition of Jackson's troops were such that every moment counted and all possible haste on our part was necessary. This forced march will never be forgotten by the survivors of Longstreet's corps.

As everyone knows we arrived in time. But before speaking of the battle that followed, the battle known as "Second Manassas," I would like to tell of something that occurred on this march which illustrates vividly the vast uncertainties of war, and shows on what little things the fate of great armies and great causes may depend. I was not concerned in it myself, except as a member of the Confederate army, but because of its interest I think I may turn aside a little from the account of my personal experiences to present it.

Colonel John Cressons, who at that time was commanding our Confederate scouts, was present and was an eyewitness. I give the story in his graphic words:

"As Hood's men, who were in the advance of Longstreet's corps, were hurrying forward to enter Thoroughfare Gap they came to a cross-roads. A mounted figure suddenly appeared, evidently a Confederate guide.

" 'This way, General Hood!' he said, gracefully saluting and pointing northward as the head of Longstreet's column swung toward the east. The guide, well mounted and wearing the uniform of a Confederate cavalryman, was at the forks of the road near the village of White Plains, in Fauquier County, Virginia.

"The road which General Hood was taking led to Thoroughfare Gap in Bull Mountain, and is the only practicable approach to the field of Manassas, where Stonewall Jackson was then struggling with the army of General Pope.

"Hood halted his column and closely questioned the guide, feeling certain that he was in error. And yet it would seem that the guide must be right. He was intelligent, confident, definite, certain of his instructions, and prompt and clear in his replies.

"He was a handsome young fellow, with bold, frank eyes and a pleasant voice, and the precision of his statements gave weight to his words.

"The situation was critical-no exigency of war could be more so. It was not merely the issue of a battle but the fate of a campaign which hung in the balance! The time was 10 a. m., August 28, 1862.

" 'Did General Jackson give you these instructions?' asked General Hood.

" 'Yes, General.'

" 'When?'

" 'About four hours ago. I left soon after sunrise.'

" 'What route did you come?'

" 'North of the mountain, General, by way of Gum Springs. There is no other road.'

" 'Do you know where Stuart is?'

" 'I saw most of his command this morning. He is pushing with his main body for Sudley, to cover Jackson's rear. The brigade has gone north to guard the trains on the Aldie Road.'

" 'Trains on the Aldie Road?' exclaimed Hood. 'What trains are you talking about?'

" 'Stonewall Jackson's trains, General. He is pushing them toward Aldie, where I supposed you would join him.'

" 'I have heard nothing of all this,' said the general.

" 'Then I'll tell you what it is, General Hood. Those devilish

Jessie Scouts****** are at it again, cutting off Stuart's couriers. Jackson has heard nothing from Longstreet since yesterday morning, and he's afraid you'll follow the old order and try to join him by Thoroughfare Gap.'

" 'Where is Jackson?' asked General Hood.

" 'I left him a little south of Sudley Springs, on the high ground commanding the turnpike.'

" 'What is he doing?'

" 'Shortening his lines, General. You see, Porter turned our right at Groveton last night, and McDowell took Thoroughfare Gap, and Pickett was sent to attack Buford's cavalry, who had seized the pass at Hopewell-at least that's what Stuart's scout told me.'

" 'You say Jackson's left is at Sudley Springs?'

" 'No, General. I intended to say that his left was *near* Sudley Springs, about a half-mile south. Kearney and Hooker attacked there in column last night, doubling us up, and the enemy now holds both the road and the ford.'

" 'But that would make Jackson's position untenable.'

" 'Yes, General, that's the reason he is falling back. They say McClellan has abandoned the James and now covers Washington, and that Burnside has arrived from the coast. Within twenty-four hours - the way they figure it - Pope will have over a hundred thousand men. When I left there at sunrise Jed Hotchkiss had all the pioneers out. He was cutting roads and clearing fords and bridging Catharpin Run, for that's the only way out now.'

" 'How did you learn all these things?' asked General Hood, and there was a note of severity in his voice.

" 'Absorbed them from the atmosphere, I suppose,' answered the guide, rather languidly.

" 'Who and what are you?' demanded General Hood, who was perplexed and anxious, yet scarcely suspicious of treachery, the guide was so bland and free and unconstrained.

" 'I am Frank Lamar, of Athens, Georgia, enrolled with the cavalry of Hampton's Legion, but now detailed on courier service at the

---

****** A famous body of Union scouts.

headquarters of Stonewall Jackson.'

" 'Where's your sabre?'

" 'I captured a handsome pistol from a Yankee officer at Port Republic and have discarded my sabre.'

" 'Let me see your pistol." It was a very fine silver-mounted Colt's revolver; one chamber was empty.

" 'When did you fire that shot?'

" 'Yesterday morning, General Hood. I shot a turkey-buzzard sitting on the fence.'

"General Hood handed the pistol to Captain Cressons, commander of scouts. Cressons scrutinized the pistol and the guide scrutinized Captain Cressons. As the captain drew General Hood's attention to the fact that the powder was still moist, showing that the pistol had been recently fired, the guide interposed, saying that he had reloaded after yesterday's practice and had fired the shot in question at another buzzard just before the column came in sight, but that he didn't suppose General Hood would be interested in such a matter.

"The guide was mistaken. General Hood was decidedly interested in the matter! Guides do not practice marksmanship when on duty between the lines.

" 'Search that man!' exclaimed General Hood, impatiently, for the general was baffled and still uncertain. All his life had been passed in active service yet this was a new experience to him.

"The search revealed strange things. In the guide's haversack were little packages of prepared coffee and blocks of condensed soup and good store of hardtack, which facts the guide pleasantly dismissed with the remark, 'It's a poor sort of Red that can't forage on the enemy.'

"The next discovery had a deeper meaning. In the lining of his vest were found the insignia of a Confederate captain, the three gold bars being secured to a base which had a thin strip of flexible steel running lengthwise through it and slightly projecting at the ends. Further search revealed minute openings in the collar of his jacket, and into these openings the devise was readily slipped and firmly held.

" 'What is the meaning of that?' asked General Hood, sternly.

"There was an air of boyish diffidence and a touch of reproach in the young man's reply. Its demure humor was half-playful, yet modest and natural, and its effect on the spectators was mainly ingratiating.

" 'Really, General Hood,' he said, 'you ask me such embarrassing questions. But I will tell you. It was just this way. Our girls, God bless them, are as devoted and patriotic as can be, but you couldn't imagine the difference they make between a commissioned officer and a private soldier.'

"Communicative as the guide was, The general could not read him. He might be an honest youth whose callow loquacity sprang from no worse a source than that of inexperience and undisciplined zeal, or be might be one of the most daring spies that ever hid supernal subtlety beneath the mask of guilelessness.

"Meanwhile the precious moments were slipping by! - the fateful moments, moments on which hung the tide of war, the fortunes of a great campaign, the door, perhaps, of a new-born nation. And there at the parting of the ways sat our boyish guide, frank, communicative, well-informed, leaning on the pommel of his saddle with the negligent grace of youth and replying with perfect good humor to all our questioning.

"We had every reason to believe that Stonewall Jackson at that moment was beset by overwhelming numbers, and nothing seemed to us more likely than that the enemy would attempt to cut off our approach by the seizure of Thoroughfare Gap. If Jackson's left flank was really at Sudley Springs and his right at Groveton, his right would be 'in the air' and a movement to turn it would virtually support an occupancy of the mountain passes. This would naturally drive Jackson northward, as our guide had stated.

"The whole situation was perilous in the extreme, and our doubts were agonizing. If the Federals occupied the pass at Thoroughfare Gap they could easily hold it against our assaults, and if Jackson should attempt to join us there they could destroy him. On the other hand, if Jackson had really retreated toward Aldie we must at once change our course and join him by a forced march northward, and to do that would be not merely to abandon the campaign as planned but also to relinquish to the enemy the short line and the open way to Richmond.

"From his first moment of misgiving General Hood had taken

measures to verify or discredit the guide's story. Swift reconnaissance was made in each direction, but the roads were ambushed by Jessie scouts and infested with detachments of Buford's cavalry. Priceless moments were thus lost, and although we felt that Stonewall Jackson must be sore beset yet we could not guess which road would take us to his battle or lead us away from it.

"Meanwhile diligent questioning went on by staff officers and couriers, the benefit of every doubt being freely accorded, for many of us believed, almost to the last, that the guide was a true man.

"When General Hood first halted his column a number of troops had strayed into the fields and woods to pick berries, and it was afterwards remembered that the guide's attention seemed to follow the soldiers, especially such of them as wandered toward a certain thicket near the edge of the forest.

"We were soon to learn the meaning of this, for in that thicket a frightful secret was hidden - a secret which, if discovered, would doom that guide to a shameful death, a death of infamy, of nameless horror, his sepulcher the gibbet, his unburied flesh a loathsome meal for those evil birds which banquet on the dead. Was there some pre-vision of this in that swift glance which he cast toward the open country as he half turned in his saddle and took a firmer grasp on the reins? There were those among us who thought so afterwards. Yet he must have known that escape by flight was impossible.

"In a moment, however, the startled gesture was gone and there was again about him that same air of negligent repose, that same tranquility of spirit, which was enhanced rather than impaired by the amused and half-scornful smile with which he regarded the scrutiny of those around him.

"While we thus observed him there was a sudden commotion among the troops. Soldiers with grave faces and some with flashing eyes were hurrying from the eastward road. They had found a dying man, a Confederate dispatch bearer, who had been dragged into the bushes and evidently left for dead. He had gasped out a few broken words, managing to say that his dispatches had been taken, torn from his breast pocket, and that he had been 'shot by one of our own men!'

"The situation now was plain enough. That pretended Southern guide was in reality a Northern spy. He had taken his life in his hand and boldly flung it into the scale of war.

"The chances against him were infinite, yet so superb was his courage, so sedate his daring, that but for those unconsidered mishaps he would have won his perilous way; he would have blasted at its fruition the matchless strategy of Lee; he would smilingly have beckoned that magnificent army to its doom!

"Never, perhaps, in all the tide of time did consequences so vast pivot upon incidents so trivial. Had General Hood followed the spy and turned to the left a certain trend of events would have been inevitable.

"Stonewall's beleaguered detachment would have perished. Longstreet's corps would have lost its base. Richmond would have fallen. John Pope would have been the nation's hero. The seat of war would have drifted toward the Gulf States, and the great tides of American history would have flowed along other courses.

"General Hood drew his brigadiers aside. The guide, or rather the spy, glanced toward them but remained unshaken. There was a certain placid fortitude in his manner which seemed incompatible with ruthless deeds. There was something of devotion in it, and self-sacrifice, relieved indeed by a touch of bravado but without a trace of fear.

"None knew better than he that that group of stern-faced men was a drumhead court, and none knew better what the award of that court would be. He had played boldly for a mighty stake. He had lost, and was ready for the penalty.

"There was a strip of forest where the roads forked, and among the trees was a large post oak with spreading branches. General Hood pointed to the tree, saying that any of its limbs would do. A Texas soldier remarked that there was no better scaffold than the back of a horse and the spy, approving the suggestion, sprang lightly up and stood on the saddle. Half a dozen men were soon busy in the tree fastening a bridle-rein at one end and adjusting a loop at the other.

"As they slipped the noose over his head the spy raised his hand impressively.

" 'Stop!' he exclaimed. 'I have three words more for you. I am neither Frank Lamar of Georgia nor Harry Brooks of Virginia. I am Jack Sterry of the Jessie Scouts. I did not kill that rebel, but I was with those that did.

" 'His dispatches by this time are safe enough! I should like my comrades to know that I palavered with your army for a good half-hour while General Pope was battering down your precious old Stonewall. Now, men, I am ready - and in parting I will simply ask you to say, if you should ever speak of this, that Jack Sterry, when the rebels got him, died as a Jessie scout should!'

"He folded his arms and his horse was led from beneath his feet. General Hood turned aside and in subdued voice gave the order of march. And the column moved on."

CHAPTER XII

SECOND MANASSAS AND SOUTH MOUNTAIN

WE reached Thoroughfare Gap in the Bull Run Mountains on the night of the 28th and passed through on the following morning. The passage was cleared by Hood's Texans after a severe fight, the enemy disputing the passage in an effort to prevent Longstreet from uniting with Jackson. This delay at the Gap allowed General Pope to concentrate his army and meet General Lee on grounds of his (Pope's) own choosing.

We found the Gap strewn with the Union dead but they had managed to carry off their wounded. We passed one of their dead lying close by on the roadside. He was a handsome lad, hardly more than eighteen years of age. His clothes were partly stripped from his body and he had the appearance of having been in the service but a few days, his flesh being so clean and fair.

On, this march, after passing through the Gap, I came to a farm house where I stopped to get some water, together with many other soldiers. I was made glad by meeting an Alexandria friend, a Mrs. Collins, who bountifully supplied me with bread and ham - this, too, at a nine when hunger was getting the best of me as food was scarce, the weather extremely hot, and water hardly obtainable.

Our regiment arrived on the field of battle tired and hungry, no rations having been issued for several days. The men had only green corn from the adjacent fields to live on. Four or five ears were allowed to each man.

At about 4 o'clock in the afternoon of the 30th our regiment, then near the Chinn House, was ordered to advance and charge the enemy's batteries, which it did, driving the enemy from that portion of the field and capturing their guns.

In this fight our regiment again suffered severely in both killed and wounded.******* Among the wounded were Colonel Corse, Lieutenant Colonel Marye, and Color Bearer Robert Steele. Private Samuel S. Coleman of Company E, captured the colors of a Union

*******See Appendix.

90

regiment, for which he was complimented in general orders. Up to this time our brigade was credited with having captured sixteen flags.

Referring to the charge Colonel Corse, who commanded Kemper's brigade in this battle, had the following to say in his official report regarding the part taken in the fighting by the Alexandria regiment:

"The Seventeenth, led by the ardent Lieutenant Colonel Marye, advanced in perfect line. Just before reaching the battery Colonel Marye fell, wounded severely (leg since amputated), and under the command of the intrepid Arthur Herbert the regiment continued the charge.

"The charge was a success. The enemy was driven from his guns, his infantry supports scattered, and his batteries taken. My line was now somewhat broken owing to the impetuosity of the charge, and seeing the enemy advancing his reserves I dispatched my assistant adjutant general, Herbert Bryant, and aid de camp Captain Beckham to you for aid, which was promptly furnished.

"Samuel Coleman, private, Company E, Seventeenth Virginia, in the hottest of the fight wrested from the hands of the color-bearer of the Eleventh Pennsylvania his regimental colors and handed them to me. These colors I have already had the honor to forward to you.

"At this juncture, having received a wound in the thigh and finding that my horse was tottering under me from a wound through the body, I turned over the command to Colonel Terry, reported to you, and with your permission retired from the field.

"Never was a brigade commander more gallantly and efficiently supported by field and company officers and brave men."

This battle was a remarkable one and of special interest because it was fought on the same ground as the First Battle of Manassas, although in this case the armies had changed position, the enemy attacking our forces from the direction of Manassas while Jackson's men were standing with their backs to Sudley Ford.

I was almost barefooted during the fight, with the soles of my shoes about ready to leave the uppers. I tried to get a pair on the field but failed, as others in a similar state were ahead of me.

We bivouacked on the field that night near the Chinn House, suffering a great deal from the wet weather and from lack of food. On

September 3 we began our march towards Leesburg. As we soon found out, we were bound for the enemy's territory. We passed through Leesburg on the 5th. While marching along Main Street we noticed a large number of horses standing in front of a residence. As we came opposite the owners came out. They proved to be General Stuart, our cavalry commander, and his staff, who were being entertained by some ladies. The ladies followed him to the sidewalk and gave him a great send-off.

Our regiment was now scarcely more than a remnant, numbering less than one hundred men. By order of the commanding general those who were without shoes had to remain in Virginia. The effect of this order was to reduce the entire strength of the army that invaded Maryland to about 35,000 men.

Our army crossed the Potomac River on the 5th and 6th by fording. The river at this point was about 350 yards wide. As General Jones commanding the old "Stonewall" division wrote, "Never had the army been so ragged, dirty, and ill provided for as on this march." Yet never were the men in better spirits. They crossed the river to the music of the popular air "Maryland, My Maryland," while their hearts beat high with hopes of new victories to be won.

On September 5 the Union forces changed commanders, General Pope being succeeded by General George B. McClellan. At this there also the two Union armies, the Army of the Potomac and the Army of Virginia, were merged under the name of the former, which name was retained until the close of the war.

The first effort on the part of our commissary to furnish us rations on our arrival in Maryland was made on September 6. It fell to my lot to receive one skein of black thread and two smoked herrings, these articles having been captured from a Union sutler. Our commissary kindly allowed us the choice of thread or buttons, and I took that which I needed most, the thread. This was the first issue of rations for about two weeks.

After marching through several small towns in Maryland we arrived at Monocacy River, where we remained two days. While here our forces destroyed the B. & O. railroad bridge over that stream.

Once while we were passing through one of the small villages we halted in front of a tavern by the roadside to enjoy one of the occasional rests allowed the troops on the march. On the porch were a number of young ladies of Union sympathies, one of whom wore an apron made to represent the Union flag.

She came boldly to the front, when some wag in our regiment proposed three cheers for the Stars and Stripes. They were given lustily and many times repeated. She stood the cheers and jests of the good-natured soldiers for a while but finally retreated into the house, followed by the cheers of the boys. During this ten-minute rest I did not hear a single ugly remark or see an act that would offend the most sensitive lady.

While on the march through the enemy country the boys would frequently indulge in the singing of their favorite camp songs. One of them ran as follows:

> "We are the boys, so gay and happy,
> Wheresoe'er we chance to be.
> If at home or on camp duty,
> 'Tis the same, we are always free.
> So let the war guns roar as they will,
> We'll be gay and happy still,
> Gay and happy, gay and happy,
> We'll be gay and happy still.
>
> "Old Virginia needs assistance,
> Northern hosts invade her soil.
> We'll present a bold resistance,
> Courting danger, death, and toil.
> So let the war guns roar as they will,
> We'll be gay and happy still,
> Gay and happy, gay and happy,
> We'll be gay and happy still."

One verse of another song which I remember went as follows:

> "Keep your shoes upon your feet,

Forward march and don't retreat.
Do you belong to the rebel band,
Fighting for your homes."

Once while the Old Dominion Rifles were whistling a lively tune and keeping step to it we passed a crowd of girls. One of them, perched upon a fence post, called out: "My Lord, you've got no music so you have to whistle to keep your courage up." She too was greeted with cheers as we marched gayly on.

On Wednesday, the 10th, we resumed our line of march, and passing through Frederick City went into bivouac near Middletown. Leaving there at 5 o'clock the next morning we marched to and through Boonsboro and Hagerstown, going into bivouac about three miles beyond Hagerstown.

Retracing our steps the next day, Friday, we passed again through Hagerstown (which is about twelve miles from Sharpsburg) to Boonsboro, where the Battle of Boonsboro, or South Mountain, was fought. Our object in contesting at this point was to give Stonewall Jackson time to accomplish his purpose, the capture of the Union forces at Harper's Ferry, and rejoin Lee for the general engagement. The fight took place near the summit of the mountain, on Sunday, September 14, 1862, and was stubbornly contested by our forces, who succeeded in holding the enemy in check until long after dark when we withdrew in good order. Major Arthur Herbert in this fight was detached from our regiment and in command of the Seventh Virginia Infantry.

I figured, much to my discomfiture, in a little occurrence during the engagement here on the mountain. Although I was present at the fight I did not participate in it, as I had been detailed that morning for duty with the field hospital corps and was put in charge of that section attached to our command. The brigade surgeon ordered me to establish the field hospital at a certain farm house nearer the battle line. To do so I had to cross a small stream at which a guard was stationed, with orders not to allow anything to cross going to the front except artillery.

The hospital train of which I had charge consisted of four wagons and twelve ambulances. On arriving at the stream I was promptly stopped by the guard. I explained my orders to him but he was firm in regard to his own orders, and would not yield. Notwithstanding, I was equally positive that my train should pass, as it was a hospital train.

How the affair would have ended I do not know, but an interruption occurred at this moment which settled it without further argument. During the dispute I had failed to notice a small group of officers on the side of the road who were listening and had overheard all that had passed. One of them intervened with the remark, "Those wagons can not cross there, sir." I looked up, and to my surprise recognized the commanding general of the army, General Lee. Imagine if you can my feelings at the moment. It is needless to say that the wagons did not cross but were turned and sent back to the rear.

What was left of our regiment, which had dwindled to forty-seven muskets and five officers, marched back through Boonsboro on to Sharpsburg. We halted in the suburbs for a short rest when many of the boys took advantage of the opportunity to do a little cooking and started a fire in the street near the curb for that purpose.

As there was no water in sight I knocked at the door of the house in front of which we were standing and asked the lady of the house as politely as I knew how if she would let me have some water so that I might make a little coffee. She refused to let me have any and the language she used in doing so was about as rough as could come from the mouth of anyone. She was simply vile. But we had some little satisfaction a moment later, for while she was still scolding us a shell fired from a Union battery which was shelling our lines from the opposite bank of the Antietam came over and knocked off the top of her chimney, scattering bricks all around, and finally burst in a basement across the street.

CHAPTER XIII

THE BATTLE OF SHARPSBURG

AFTER Appomattox, as one writer tells it, General Lee was asked by a prominent lady of Alexandria which battle he felt proudest of, and he answered, "Sharpsburg, for I fought against greater odds there than in any other battle of the war."

In this fight, the bloodiest of the war considering the number engaged, General McClellan reported over 87,000 men for duty on the field that day. General Lee had less than 37,000 of all arms, and he remained on the field all the day following the battle waiting for the enemy to attack. But they did not do so.

The battlefield of Sharpsburg was less than four miles in length from right to left, running north and south, and less than two miles wide. In this small space of two miles by four one can well imagine what it would mean to have 125,000 men with 469 pieces of artillery fighting continuously for eighteen hours.

The Confederate line stretched from the bend on Antietam Creek, south of Burnside Bridge (near which we were stationed), north almost to Dunbar's Mill, then northwest to the Potomac. It ran about two miles to the left of Sharpsburg and about one mile to the right. The left was under General Jackson and the right under Longstreet.

Our brigade, Kemper's, from which the Seventh and Twenty-fourth Regiments had been detached and sent to other points, leaving only the First, Eleventh, and our own Seventeenth Regiments, was at the extreme right of Lee's army, with nothing beyond our right except cavalry posted to report any attempt at a flank movement.

Our position was just on the edge of the town limits, where we remained until about 3:30 o'clock on the afternoon of Wednesday, the 17th, when the enemy's line was reported advancing. Kemper's brigade was advanced to meet them. And then followed one of the most terrible battles in which our command had ever taken part - a battle in which our men courageously held their own until compelled by vastly superior numbers to retire.

The main outlines of this battle on our front, as told by various writers, can be briefly given.

General Burnside of the Union army, with his corps of 14,000 men, had been lying all day beyond the bridge which now bears his name. Ordered to cross at 8 o'clock and again at noon, he managed to get over by 3 o'clock in the afternoon and was then ready to advance, having allowed General Toombs, with less than 400 men, to delay the crossing of his Ninth Corps for three hours. It is said that had he followed Napoleon's tactics at Arcola and rushed his men across the bridge he would have ended the war then and there. But it is also said that McClellan's dispatch early on the morning of the 17th ordering him to hold the bridge ("If the bridge is lost all is lost") made him over-cautious.

Once across the bridge he moved against the hill which General D. R. Jones, commanding our little division of 2,500, was holding. Longstreet was watching this advance. Jackson was at General Lee's headquarters on a knoll in rear of Sharpsburg. A. P. Hill was coming but had not arrived, and it was apparent that Burnside must be stayed, if at all, with artillery.

Burnside's heavy line moved up the hill, and, as an eye-witness said, the earth seemed to tremble beneath their tread. It was a splendid and fearful sight, but for that large force to beat back Jones' feeble line was scarcely war. The artillery tore but did not stay them. They pressed forward until Sharpsburg was uncovered, and Lee's line of retreat was it their mercy.

But then, just then, A. P. Hill, picturesque in his red battle shirt, who had marched that day seventeen miles in eight hours from Harper's Ferry and had waded the Potomac and crossed the Antietam by the lower bridge, appeared upon the scene. Without waiting for orders he attacked, striking the Union forces in flank with 3,000 bayonets.

Tired and footsore, his men forgot their woes in that supreme moment and with no breathing time braced themselves for the coming shock. They met it, and stayed it. The blue line staggered and hesitated, and hesitating was lost.

At the critical moment A. P. Hill was always at his strongest. Quickly advancing his battle-flags he moved his line forward. Jones' troops rallied on him, and in din of musketry and artillery an either flank

97

the Federals broke and ran over the fields. Hill did not wait for his other brigades but held the vantage gained until Burnside was driven back to the Antietam and under the shelter of heavy guns. The day was done.

Such was the bloody Battle of Sharpsburg, or at least that part of it which took place on our front, as the historian sees it. To the man in the ranks it had a far more exciting aspect. I am fortunate in being able to present the battle events as seen through the eyes of the members of our sadly depleted old Seventeenth. Soon after the war Mr. Alexander Hunter, a member of Company A of the Seventeenth Virginia, wrote a graphic account of this fight on the right of our line, and I can not do better than to give his thrilling description:

"At dawn of the fateful morning of September 17 we reached the little village of Sharpsburg, and forming in line of battle just on the right of where the National Cemetery is now located we lay down and slept like logs, though the fight at the Dunkards' Church on our left was raging in all its fury.

"We moved several times in the course of the day but at noon the final position was selected behind a post-and-rail fence near where we first stopped. The order to halt was given, the line formed, and the command to stack arms rang out. I was the only private left in Company A and having no comrade to lock bayonets with I ran mine into the ground.

"The only officer left in my company was Lieutenant Tom Perry. A mild-mannered, slow-speaking man was but he was a soldier, every inch of him. He never made a boast in his life but in every battle in which the Seventeenth was engaged there in front of his company stood Tom, calm and serene, as if waiting for the dinner horn to blow.

"Longstreet's old First Brigade, that which charged through the abattis at Seven Pines 2,800 strong, mustered only 320 men. The Seventeenth Virginia, the pride of Alexandria, Prince William, Fairfax, Fauquier, Loudoun, and Warren Counties, which at Blackburn's Ford had 860 men in ranks, now stood in their tracks with forty-seven muskets and five officers. * * *

"About noon we were ordered to fall in, and in a few moments Toombs' skeleton brigade took position on the bluff overlooking Antietam Bridge.

"Burnside had commenced his attack. Just at this moment a battery dashed by us, the Rockbridge Artillery, and I had only time to wave my hand at my old schoolfellow Bob Lee, a private in the battery and son of our commander-in-chief, when it disappeared down the hill.

"And then Toombs got to work in earliest. No words can describe the gallant fight he made to keep Burnside from crossing the bridge. Again and again he drove back the blue columns, with nothing behind him for support. The Georgians fought on until their gun barrels were too hot for the naked hands.

"On our left it seemed as if Hades had broken loose. The volleys of musketry and noise of the artillery were mingled in one vast roar that shook the earth - and this kept up for nearly two hours.

"The whole of our front and left was wrapped in an impenetrable cloud of smoke. Then came a lull, and I was sent to the village with canteens to get water. I had a clear view from the steeple of a church which I climbed, and then hurried back and said to Colonel Corse of my regiment:

" 'We are lost, Colonel! We haven't a single reserve.'

" 'Is it possible?' he exclaimed.

"I told him it was a fact. There was not a solitary Confederate soldier in sight. He clenched his teeth like a bull- dog, and as the news spread along the line each man knew we had to stay there, and if needs be, die there. As we lay there waiting for the attack that all knew must come, every man in the ranks wondered why it was delayed.

"I had seen from my perch in the town that there was a great force of Federals near Burnside Bridge and that our thin line could not stand long against a determined attack. Our attention was given to the fighting on our left, which had broken out with redoubled fury.

"About 3 p. m. we received a shock, for the remains of Toombs' Georgians came tearing down the hill, and then all the batteries across the bridge opened and swept the hill where we were lying. Every one of our batteries limbered up and returned, leaving the single line of infantry to brave the storm.

"In about a half-hour it came. Then the artillery was silent, and the infantrymen who had lain there face downward, exposed to the iron hail, now arose, placed their cartridge boxes in position, rested their muskets on the lower rail, and with clenched teeth, fast-beating hearts, and hurried breath braced themselves for the shock.

"The fence was not built on the top of the hill but some fifty feet from the crest. Consequently we could not see the attacking force until they were within pistol shot of us. We could hear the *'rat-a-plan'* of their drums, the stern commands of their officers, the muffled sound of marching feet.

"Colonel Corse gave but one order: 'Don't fire, men, until I give the word.'

"As we lay there with our eyes ranging along the musket barrels, our fingers on the trigger, we saw the gilt eagles on the flag-poles emerge over the top of the hill, followed by the flags drooping on the staffs. Then the tops of the caps appeared, and next a line of the fiercest eyes men ever looked upon. We heard the shouts of the officers urging their men forward.

"Less brave, less seasoned troops would have faltered before the array of deadly tubes levelled at them, and the recumbent line, silent, motionless and terrible. But if there was any giving way we did not see it.

"They fired at us before we pulled trigger and came on with vibrant shouts. Not until they were well up in view did Colonel Corse break the silence, and his voice was a shriek as he ordered: 'Fire!'

"All the guns went off at once. The whole brigade fire seemed to follow our volley, and the enemy's line, sadly thinned, broke and went over the hill. Every man in our line began to load his musket with frenzied haste. Only a few of the Seventeenth were shot, the fire of the enemy having been too high.

"We had hardly loaded and capped the muskets when the blue line came with a rush, and we fired now without orders. Before we could load a third time, the two lines of battle of the Federals, now commingled as one solid bank of men, poured a volley into us that settled the matter. It killed or wounded every man in the regiment except seven, of whom I was fortunate to be one.

"Just as the bluecoats were climbing the fence I threw down my musket and raised my hands in token of surrender. Two or three stopped to carry me back to the rear and the rest kept on, urged by their

100

officers, in the direction of the village of Sharpsburg. Major Herbert and Lieutenant Perry made a dash for the rear and escaped. I and a private named Gunnell, of the Fairfax Rifles, were the only prisoners taken. The rest of the regiment lay there motionless in their positions. The men were either lying down or kneeling; the wounds were dangerous or deadly.

"But for the protection afforded by the fence I do not believe that a single man of the regiment would have escaped alive. In conversation with Dr. McGill, of Hagerstown, Maryland, shortly after the war I was told that two days after the battle he visted [sic] the spot, having had some friends in the Alexandria regiment of Kemper's brigade. He said that the fence was literally a thing of shreds and patches.

"Our captors hurried us off. When we reached a hill in the rear we stopped to rest. My captors said to me, 'It's all up with you, Johnnie. Look there!'

"I turned and gazed on the scene. Long lines of blue were coming like surging billows of the ocean. The bluecoats were wild with excitement, and their measured hurrah, so different from our piercing yell, rose above the thunder of their batteries beyond the bridge. I thought the guard was right, that it was all up with us and our whole army would be captured.

"We, Yank and Reb, were sitting down taking a sociable smoke when all at once we were startled as if touched by an electric shock.

"The air was filled with bursting shells, as if a half-dozen batteries had opened at once from the direction of Sharpsburg. While we stood gazing we saw emerging from a cornfield a long line of gray, musket barrels scintillating in the rays of the declining sun and the Southern battle-flags gleaming redly against the dark background.

"They seemed to have struck the Federal advance on the flank. From the long line of gray a purplish mist broke, pierced here and there by a bright gleam, and the noise of the volley sounded like the whir of machinery.

"In an instant the whole scene was changed. The triumphant advance, the jubilant shouts, the stirring beat of the drums, the mad, eager rush of the forces in blue were stayed, and back they came, without order or formation. We joined the hurrying throng, not stopping until we reached the valley near the bridge.

"The attacking force was that of General A. P. Hill. It was Stonewall Jackson who saved the Army of Northern Virginia from disastrous defeat, as he had done at the First Manassas, at the Seven Days' Battles at Richmond, and later on at Chancellorsville."

When the charge of the Federals forced us back we had had to abandon the two pieces of artillery we had with us on the line and these guns, together with our wounded, among whom was Colonel Corse, fell into the possession of the enemy. But it was only for a short time, as our return to our position was so quick that we recovered them all.

This repulse of the Federals of Burnside's corps ended the fighting on our front and it was not resumed on the following day. We remained in position until the afternoon of the 18th when we left the lines and marched to the river, a distance of about three miles. We crossed at a ford about one mile below Shepherdstown, wading the stream, which was quite deep and extremely cold.

Among the severely wounded in the battle was William J. Hall, my closest companion in the army. He had been shot in four places, two of his wounds being double, and at the time he was supposed to be mortally hurt. Hall was greatly beloved. I remember well the scene on the battlefield that night when Major Arthur Herbert with the seven survivors, all that was left of our regiment, knelt by the side of the litter on which Hall was lying and offered up a prayer.

I managed to place him in a barn about two hundred yards in the rear of where he fell and remained with him all night. When we crossed the river the next day I was ordered by Major Herbert to take charge of the wounded and see to transporting them to Virginia soil, rather a difficult task because of the high water, which came up several inches into the ambulances. The one in which we had placed Hall was forced by the passing troops out of the regular fording place on to a rocky path on the side, where the wheels became wedged in the rocks. We released it with great difficulty and then only through the aid of some artillerymen whom I called to our assistance.

We finally reached the Virginia shore in safety and I succeeded in getting him into a vacant storeroom which had been converted into a temporary hospital. I was compelled to leave and join my command and I left him in the care of those who had charge of the place.

After I had gone someone who knew him came in and covered him with a sheet. On it they pinned a card giving his name and regiment and requesting that whoever buried the body would please mark the spot.

It happened soon after that a lady and her two daughters came in with the intention of taking to their home some one of the wounded and caring for him. They read and commented on the inscription and were passing on when the hoopskirt of one of the young ladies caught on the handle of the litter and shook it. From under the sheet came a groan and when they removed the sheet they found, to their astonishment, a live Confederate soldier.

They obtained permission to take him to their home and had him immediately removed. There through gentle nursing at the hands of these kind ladies and through the attentions of one of the surgeons who had been left in charge of our wounded he was again restored to health. He died in Washington on February 22, 1926, leaving me as the sole survivor of Company H, the Old Dominion Rifles, which sixty-five years before had left Alexandria one hundred and eleven strong.

In writing of this campaign which ended in the Battle of Sharpsburg the Union officer General George B. Davis says:

"The management of the Army of the Potomac was halting, dilatory, wanting in fine direction, and to a degree irresolute and unskilful. From beginning to end of the campaign the Confederate commander's conduct was characterized by boldness, resolution, and quickness; the Federal commander's by timidity, irresolution, and slowness."

Comment on the Battle of Sharpsburg itself usually emphasizes the fierce fighting and the heavy casualties. " It was a stand-up, hand-to-hand fight," says Major Hotchkiss, of Jackson's staff, "as brave and furious as any the world ever saw, and in it the Confederate soldiers proved themselves more than a match, in a fair and open conflict, for their Federal foes." General Alexander terms it "the bloodiest battle ever fought on this continent," and Mr. John C. Ropes, in his able review of the battle, says that "it is likely that more men were killed and wounded on that 17th day of September than on any other single day of the war."

These views are largely supported by the records which show, among other things, that no less than eight Union generals and commanders were killed and eleven wounded, and that five Confederate generals were killed and six wounded, or a total of thirty casualties on both sides among officers of this grade.

The losses in my own regiment, the Seventeenth Virginia, have been mentioned several times as an example of how severe was the fighting at Sharpsburg. Colonel Henderson in his "Life of Stonewall Jackson" and Mrs. General George Pickett in her history of "Pickett and His Men", among other writers, tell how the regiment went into battle with a strength of between fifty-five and sixty men and officers and came out with only seven unhurt.[*] Among the wounded were the colonel of the regiment, M. D. Corse, and the adjutant, Herbert Bryant.

The question has frequently been asked why the Seventeenth Virginia carried so few men into this fight at Sharpsburg? It is easily answered.

The reader will remember that our regiment went into its first battle at Bull Run with about 865 men. We lost quite a number in the trenches at Yorktown. Then on May 5, at the Battle of Williamsburg, we lost heavily, about thirty per cent of the number engaged. In a little over three weeks from that date, on May 30, we were thrown into battle at Seven Pines, where we lost over seventy killed and wounded. Thirty days later, on June 30, we fought the Battle of Frazier's Farm where our loss in killed, wounded, and missing was over one hundred.

Then on August 30, two months later, followed the Second Battle of Manassas where we again suffered severely. We went on into Maryland and lost a few more at Boonsboro, or South Mountain. When all these losses are taken into account and when allowance is also made for the large number that could not accompany the army into Maryland because of being barefooted it can easily be seen why we went into the Battle of Sharpsburg with barely a handful of men and why, for a while, the regiment was practically wiped out as an organization.

The heavy losses it sustained in this latest battle would be good

---

[*]See Appendix.

proof of the valor of the regiment, if any were needed. But at Sharpsburg, as at the Second Manassas, it came out of the battle with a visible trophy to testify to its fighting qualities in the shape of a flag captured from the enemy. The presentation of these two flags to the Secretary of War was made the occasion for a letter from the Commanding General, calling special attention to the record of the regiment and its commander. This letter, written about five weeks after Sharpsburg, was as follows:

"Headquarters Army of Northern Virginia
October 23, 1862.
"Hon. George W. Randolph,
Secretary of War.

"Sir: I have the honor to transmit with the accompanying letter of Brigadier General James L. Kemper two stands of colors captured from the United States forces by the Seventeenth Virginia Regiment at the battles of Manassas and Sharpsburg.

"This regiment, with its gallant colonel (M. D. Corse), who in the words of General Longstreet 'have been distinguished in at least ten of the severest battles of the war,' challenge the admiration of their countrymen.

"The United States national flag was taken by Private Samuel S. Coleman, of the Mount Vernon Guards, from the color-sergeant of the Eleventh Pennsylvania Regiment in the Battle of Manassas, August 30.

"The regimental flag of the One Hundred and Third New York Volunteers was captured by Lieutenant W. W. Athey in the battle of Sharpsburg, September 17, 1862.

"The names of the captors are appended to the colors, respectively, and I hope will be preserved with them.
"I have the honor to be
"Your obedient servant,
"R. E. Lee,
General Commanding."

In connection with the capture of this flag at Sharpsburg by the Seventeenth Virginia from the New York regiment directly in front of it, the fact is worth noting that General Fairchild, commander of the Union forces engaged there, failed to mention the capture in his report made a few days later. Even General McClellan in a report made twelve days after the battle states:

"We have not lost a single gun or flag in the Battle of Antietam."

The memory of these commanders, however, evidently failed them. On several occasions I have visited the magnificent museum in the New York State Capitol, at Albany, and in the space allotted to the One Hundred and Third New York Regiment of Infantry have seen a beautiful regimental flag which had been presented to that command by the City Council of New York when it entered the service. The flag had attached to it a card with the following inscription:

"Flag of the 103rd New York Regiment, Colonel Fairchilds, captured at the Battle of Sharpsburg, September 17, 1862, by Lieutenant W. W. Athey, Company C, Seventeenth Virginia Infantry, Confederate States Army. Recaptured by us at the fall of Richmond."

Incidentally, in the same museum is the flag taken from the roof of the Marshall House in our city on May 24, 1861, by Colonel Ellsworth, and in the same case with it is the colonel's full uniform.

CHAPTER XIV

CONDITION AND DISCIPLINE OF LEE'S ARMY

MUCH has been written and said about the condition and equipment of our army, and its morale and conduct (especially while in enemy territory) in this campaign of 1862 and later. I think it will be fitting to give here a number of brief comments on those matters from men who were in a good position to know about them. The comments are from men both within and outside of the ranks, and from both Confederate and Union sympathizers, as well as neutral observers.

I have mentioned several times some of the hardships we experienced, especially in the month or two previous to fighting the Battle of Sharpsburg. My comrade of the Seventeenth, Mr. Alexander Hunter, whose description of that battle I have given in the last chapter, has also told of these privations in words much more vivid than I can command, and I will again borrow a short passage from his writings:

"I doubt if any army on earth endured greater hardships or went through more than Lee's army in the late summer and early fall of 1862.

"On August 18 of that year our brigade, composed of the First, Seventh, Eleventh, Seventeenth, and Twenty-fourth Virginia Infantry, set its face northward from Gordonsville. Every knapsack and all camp equipage were left behind and in light marching order, with sixty rounds of ammunition, a blanket over our shoulders, and five days' rations in our haversacks, we headed for the Rapidan River.

"Those five days' rations, which lasted us two days, were the last we drew for nearly two weeks. The forced march of August 28 and 29 to aid Jackson was a fearful ordeal, made as it was in the intense heat with the roads deep in dust. But we reached Thoroughfare Gap in time, passed through following Hood, and on the next day fought the Second Battle of Manassas.

"Our men were so hungry that they gathered the crackers and meat from the haversacks of the dead Federals and ate as they fought. The next day we kept on to Chantilly and fought there, and then, swinging to Leesburg, we struck for the Potomac.

"In all these days we had no change of clothing and we were

literally devoured by vermin. We had no tents and we slept on the open ground - and slept soundly, even though the rain was pouring in torrents. A prize fighter trains about two months to get himself in perfect condition. But we had been training in a more vigorous manner for two years, and the men were skin, bone, and muscle.

"We lived on apples and green corn all of this time, and the soldiers began to drop out of the ranks at every halt. Then an order came for the barefooted men to remain behind and report in Winchester. Every step our army made northward it became weaker.

"At last we stood on the long-dreamed-of banks of the Potomac, and 'Maryland, my Maryland' met our gaze at last. Truly it shone -

"Fair as the garden of the Lord
To the famished eyes of the rebel horde.'

"With a rush and a swing we passed through the 'loyal' city of Frederick, where we got scant welcome, up the dusty, broad pike northward to Hagerstown, where the people received the ragged 'Rebs' as if they were belted knights with victory on their plumes. Here every soldier got as much as he could eat.

"Then came the long roll and we fell into ranks and sorrowfully turned our faces southward, and went with a swinging gait towards the mountains to help General D. H. Hill. We reached Crampton's Gap after the fight was over, then retraced our steps and on the morning of the 16th of September lighted on the fields of Boonsboro, tired and oh, so hungry!

"Apples and corn, corn and apples, were our only fare. We ate them raw, roasted, boiled together, and fried. They served to sustain life, and that was all.

"I have often been asked about the 'Rebel yell'. I have always answered that the Rebs were savage with hunger, and men always 'holler' when hungry.***

"My, my, what a set of ragamuffins they (the members of the Seventeenth Virginia) looked! It seemed as if every cornfield in Maryland had been robbed of its scarecrows and propped up against that fence.

"None had any underclothing. My costume consisted of a pair

of ragged trousers, a stained, dirty jacket, and an old hat, the brim pinned up with a thorn. A begrimed blanket over my shoulder, a greased, smeared cotton haversack full of apples and corn, a cartridge box full, and a musket completed my outfit. I was bare-footed and had stone bruises on each foot.

"Some of my comrades were a little better dressed, some were worse. I was the average. But there was not one there who would not have been 'run in' by the police had he appeared on the streets of any populous city, and fined next day for undue exposure.

"Yet these grimy, sweaty, lean, ragged men were the flower of Lee's army. These tattered, starving, unkempt fellows were the pride of their sections. These were the men -

'Whose ancestors followed Smith along the sands
And Raleigh around the seas'."

Bearing out this testimony are the official records and letters from high officers, including those of General Robert E. Lee. On November 14, 1862, a communication to the War Department, for information of the Secretary, said that "General Lee desires to state that in Pickett's division alone there are 2,071 barefooted." In the same month Longstreet's corps reported 6,648 men without any covering for their feet. But fortunately for them it was not the dead of winter.

Two months later, however, there was plenty of winter, with much snow and cold, and the same conditions prevailed. Writing to his Congressman in January, 1863, a Louisiana officer told how, out of 1,500 men reported for duty, 400 were totally without covering of any kind for their feet, the Fifth Regiment could not drill for want of shoes, and the Eighth Regiment would soon be unable to do so for the same reason. Even when shoes should be supplied the men would be unable to wear them for a long while, such was the condition of their feet. A large number of men were without a single blanket, and some had not a particle of underclothing, while overcoats were objects of curiosity. He said further that the troops had no tents and were almost totally unprovided with cooking utensils for the petty rations they received.

General Lee, writing to his wife in October, 1863, said that thousands were barefooted, thousands more had only fragments of shoes, and all were without overcoats, blankets, or warm clothing. Later on, in writing to the Secretary of War, he said that only fifteen in one regiment had shoes and that bacon was issued only once in several days. On one occasion he said that the troops were in line of battle three days, exposed to the severities of the winter, without a particle of meat. In January, 1864, he wrote to the Quartermaster General at Richmond that a brigade which had recently gone on picket had been compelled to leave several hundred men in camp because they could not bear the exposure of duty, having no shoes or blankets.

Speaking for myself, I recall that while passing through Frederick City, Maryland, with my command I noticed two men standing on the sidewalk calling the attention of some ladies to my condition.

I was not entirely shoeless, for I had the soles of my shoes held to the uppers by pieces of bandages, which I had to renew quite often. But I was good and ragged, all right! My hat I had found at a farmhouse in Virginia. It was part of a straw that had been painted or varnished black, and half of the rim was missing. It took the place of a good brown felt hat that I had up to within a few days of our entering on Maryland soil and that I lost one night when, tired and footsore, I was allowed by the driver of one of the wagons of our regiment to get in and ride. Crawling out just before daybreak I found that my hat was missing. It had evidently fallen out during the night.

Referring to the condition of our army at this time, when we entered the enemy's territory, a Union clergyman who was in Frederick City at the time wrote to Governor Curtin, of Pennsylvania, that he saw all of Lee's army that passed through that city on September 10 on its way to Sharpsburg, and that "they were ragged and shoeless, but full of fight."

And now a few words concerning the discipline in our army, about which much has been written.

Later on in the war a northern writer had this to say with respect to the impressions made upon him by Lee's troops when they pushed into Maryland:

"The Confederate army, as they marched through our country, presented a solid front. They came in close marching order, the different brigades, divisions, and corps all within supporting distance of each other. Their dress consisted of nearly every imaginable color and style, the butternut predominating. Some had blue blouses which they had doubtless stripped from the Union dead. Hats, or the skeletons of what had been hats, surmounted their poorly covered heads.

"Many were ragged and shoeless, affording unmistakable evidence that their wardrobe sadly needed to be replenished. They were, however, all well armed and *under perfect discipline.* They seemed to move as one vast machine. Laughing, talking, singing, and cheering were not indulged in, and straggling was scarcely seen."

The same writer, in referring to the order of General Lee that private property was to be respected, said: "Candor compels me to say that in the main these humane regulations were observed."

Field Marshal Wolseley, of the British army, who visited us in the fall of 1862 and witnessed all inspection of our army under Lee, said:

"I have seen many armies file past in all the pomp of fresh clothing and well-polished accoutrements, but I never saw one composed of finer men or looking more like business than that portion of General Lee's army which I was fortunate to see inspected."

Colonel Freemantle, also of the British army, who was with our army the next year in its invasion of Pennsylvania, said:

"I saw no straggling into the houses, nor were any of the inhabitants disturbed or annoyed by the soldiers. I went into Chambersburg again and witnessed the singular good behavior of the troops towards the citizens. To one who has seen, as I have, the ravages of the Northern troops in Southern towns this forbearance seems most commendable and surprising."

General Joseph E. Hooker, who succeeded Burnside in command of the Union army and who commanded at the Battle of Chancellorsville at the time when Jackson was mortally wounded, claimed at the time that he commanded "an army of veterans, the finest on the planet." Yet in his testimony before the Congressional Committee on the Conduct of the War he made the following explanation of his defeat and failure to conquer the Army of Northern Virginia.

"Our artillery had always been superior to that of the rebels, as was also our infantry, *except in discipline;* and that, for reasons not necessary to mention, *never did equal Lee's army, which has, by discipline alone, acquired a character for steadiness and efficiency unsurpassed, in my judgment, in ancient or modern times.* We have not been able to rival it, nor has there been any near approximation to it in the other rebel armies."

These statements, coming from the authorities they do, should put at rest the many reports that Lee and his generals were commanding only armed mobs.

An army correspondent, writing to a Northern journal his account of the "shameful" defeat of Hooker by the ragged rebels, describes in the following overdrawn lines the kind of troops by whom it was done:

"We had men enough, well enough equipped and well enough posted, to have devoured the ragged, imperfectly armed and equipped host of our enemies from off the face of the earth.

"Their artillery horses are poor, starved frames of beasts, tied on to their carriages and caissons with odds and ends of rope and strips of rawhide. Their supply and ammunition trains look like a congregation of all the crippled California emigrant trains that ever escaped off the desert out of the clutches of the rampaging Comanche Indians. The men are ill-dressed, ill-equipped, and ill-provided - a set of ragamuffins, that a man is ashamed to be seen among, even when he is a prisoner and can't help it.

"And yet they have beaten us fairly, beaten us all to pieces, beaten us so easily that we are objects of contempt even to their commonest private soldiers, who have no shirts to hang out of the holes in their pantaloons, and whose cartridge boxes are tied round their waists with strands of rope."

A Union officer writing at this time said: "It is beyond all wonder how men such as the rebel troops are can fight as they do. That those ragged wretches, sick, hungry, and in all ways miserable, should prove such heroes in a fight is past explanation."

In commenting on General Hooker's boastful order to his army on the eve of the Battle of Chancellorsville, General Carl Schurz, of the Union army, said: "It jarred upon my feelings as well as my good sense to hear my commanding general boast of having the enemy in the hollow

112

of his hand, that enemy being Robert E. Lee at the head of the best infantry in the world."

Finally, Charles Francis Adams, a brigadier general in the Union army, wrote: "Speaking deliberately, having faced some portions of the Army of Northern Virginia, I do not believe that any more formidable or better organized or animated force was ever set in motion than that which Lee led over the Potomac."

To these testimonials I may add one little item from my personal observations which shows what a spirit of discipline and self-restraint prevailed in our army.

On our entry into Sharpsburg we found standing on the main street a flag-pole on which was flying the Stars and Stripes. Notwithstanding the fact that we held possession of the town for several days, the flag was not disturbed. We left it flying when we evacuated the place.

In connection with this matter of the flag I may add a little postscript. A good many years after the war, accompanied by my old comrade, William J. Hall, I visited the battlefield of Sharpsburg. We were joined there by Captain J. V. Davis, then in charge of the Antietam National Cemetery located on the edge of the town, and also by the superintendent of the battlefield. While the superintendent was in his house, where he had gone for a few minutes to change his coat, I told Captain Davis about the flag. He doubted my story, saying he did not believe we would have left it flying but that we would have had both the pole and the flag down in a hurry. But when the superintendent returned I repeated the story to him and he confirmed it, stating as a fact that the flag was not disturbed by the Confederates.

CHAPTER XV

FREDERICKSBURG AND AFTER

AFTER crossing the Potomac we had a short rest near Shepherdstown and then marched again, taking the road leading in the direction of Martinsburg. We encamped at Big Spring, about two miles from that town.

While we were in camp near Martinsburg the army was reorganized. Pickett's and Kemper's Virginia brigades and Jenkins' South Carolina brigade were consolidated into a division and Brigadier General Pickett was assigned to its command. The strength of the division was about 9,000. On October 10, 1862, Brigadier General Pickett was promoted to the rank of major general and was placed permanently in command of the division designated by his name.

On taking command General Pickett appointed the following Alexandrians to positions at headquarters: Captain W. Douglas Stuart as chief engineer, Raymond Fairfax as chief of pioneer corps, Harris Hough as chief clerk, and Richard Avery as assistant chief clerk. The two last-named were transferred from the Alexandria Riflemen. Later on, while at Petersburg in 1863, Surgeon M. M. Lewis was made chief surgeon of the division.

We remained at Martinsburg several days but eventually moved in the direction of Winchester, that loyal town, and then on towards Front Royal, fording the Shenandoah on our way.

In his history of the Army of Northern Virginia Mr. George Wise of this city tells of a little episode that occurred while we were quietly encamped here in the Valley. It reflected credit on one of our Alexandria officers and is worth retelling here.

General Lee sent for Major George Duffey of Alexandria and asked for the loan of a pair of spurs, saying he had lost his own. Major Duffey complied with the request and then told the general that he would have a pair made for him.

Major Duffey gathered the necessary materials and superintended the manufacture of a pair of silver spurs which came as near to being an ideal set as he could make it. Then he carried them in all their beauty to headquarters and presented them to General Lee, who accepted them with every evidence of appreciative admiration.

The presentation was made in the presence of several English gentlemen, visitors to the Army of Northern Virginia. Among them was Sir Garret Wolseley, who seemed very deeply interested in the unique beauty of the gift. After each gentleman had thoroughly and critically examined the spurs one of the Englishmen asked General Lee:

"Are they not imported ?"

"Ah, gentlemen," he replied, "you think we are poor rebels and barbarians. You make a mistake. They were not only made in the Confederacy but here on this field, with the rough tools we use in repairing artillery and small arms."

Leaving this camp we passed through the town of Front Royal, crossed the mountain at Chester's Gap, and on October 31 reached Culpeper Court House, where we remained until November 21. Then we took up our march to Fredericksburg and made twenty-two miles in one day. This brought us near that town and we again went into camp.

On one of our long marches down the Valley, hungry, tired, nearly worn out, and hoping every minute that we might stop and go into bivouac, I happened to notice among a number of wagons parked on the roadside one marked 8th Louisiana. I knew it belonged to Hay's brigade, of Jackson's command. My father was attached to this brigade as forage master. I asked one of the men standing near if my father was anywhere about, and the men pointed to a nearby campfire, where I saw him about to sit down to his supper. It was a joyful sight to me. He had just returned from a foraging expedition and had been able to collect some food different from that which was being issued to the troops. Needless to say, after supper I left him feeling much refreshed and with a well-filled haversack. I soon caught up with my regiment, which had gone into bivouac.

General Burnside, who was now in command of the Union army, was busy putting his forces in position on Stafford Heights, on the opposite side of the Rappahannock River.

While here at this camp we learned of the promotion of our gallant colonel to the grade of brigadier general. The appointment was made November 1, 1862. What might have been a sad loss to us was made bright by the fact that we were to remain with him in the new brigade to be formed, which was to consist of the Fifteenth, Seventeenth, Thirtieth, and Thirty-second Virginia Regiments. The new brigade went into camp December 3, 1862. Lieutenant Colonel Morton Marye became the colonel of our regiment and Major Arthur Herbert the lieutenant colonel, while Captain R. H. Simpson, of Company B, became major.

The boys of the Old Dominion Rifles felt proud of their company, which had furnished the service with a brigadier general and the regiment with a lieutenant colonel, both of whom were former captains of the company. No other company of the regiment had such a record.

The weather was very severe, and the ground was covered with snow. But we were in a comfortable camp, with nothing to worry us but the movements of the enemy, who was busy throwing up heavy works on the other side of the river. However, about 3:40 o'clock on the morning of Thursday, December 11, while I was lying in my tent with W. C. Milburn, my sleeping companion at that time, I was aroused by the signal guns fired on Lee's Hill.

I woke Milburn and told him that we would soon be ordered out as the guns evidently meant a move of some kind. We had but a short time to wait when a courier dashed up, inquiring for the general's tent. I directed him to it. It was then nearing 4 o'clock and as dark as Erebus. A moment or two later our drummer, Jack Nightingill, gave us the long roll, which was repeated throughout all the camps.

The army was now on the move. We moved out and took position on the line of battle below Fredericksburg. When Friday morning dawned the enemy had succeeded in throwing over additional pontoons and the Union army was nearly over.

The enemy began their advance with an attempt to cross the river in front of the town, but they were held in check by General Barksdale and his Mississippians until our troops could get into position. On the morning of Friday, December 12, General Lee's entire force was in position, ready to receive the attack of the Union army.

Saturday morning opened cloudy, with a heavy fog enveloping the plain before us. Near noon the sun came out and the fog disappeared, disclosing the long, dark lines of the enemy in our front. The position of our command was such that we had a splendid view of the fight without participating in it.

The battle was truly a grand spectacle to witness. The long lines of the enemy, two deep, crossed the broad plain and charged our lines, attacking Hood's division on the right of us, which was posted just in the edge of the woods. Charge after charge was made and as often repulsed, and each time such a shout went up along the whole line as almost to drown out the roar of the musketry. Night closed the battle, the enemy falling back along the whole front, defeated.

Sunday and Monday passed quietly, but on Tuesday morning, the 16th, we found that the enemy had availed itself of the darkness of the night and the raging of a violent storm of wind and rain to steal away, and that it was safe back on the heights of Stafford on the opposite bank of the Rappahannock.

The official report, as published by the United States authorities, states that the Army of the Potomac, commanded by General Burnside, on this occasion had an "aggregate present for duty" of 132,017 officers and men, not including cavalry. The Army of Northern Virginia, under the command of General Lee, had an aggregate of 69,391, not including cavalry.

A few days after this battle we moved our camp near Guinea Station, about eighteen miles below Fredericksburg. Here we went into winter quarters.

On January 27, 1863, we were ordered out in a drenching cold rain which continued all day. The troops marched about fifteen miles over miserable roads and finally went into bivouac in a pine forest near Salem Church. During the night the storm continued, changing into a snowstorm. The winds howled about us. Many trees were torn up by the roots, endangering the lives of the men. We were without tents or shelter other than that which we made for ourselves with blankets or boughs of trees, and we were compelled to lie down to rest drenched to the skin. Snow fell to a depth of eight inches. The suffering at this time among the troops was something fearful, so destitute were they of shoes, clothing, and tents.

On the following morning a heavy detail was made from our

regiment to proceed about a mile and a half from camp and throw up breastworks. I was on this detail. This project was soon abandoned on account of the severity of the storm and the changed movements of the enemy, and early on the morning of the next day we were on our return to our old camp near Guinea Station.

On our way we passed many wagons disabled or buried in the muddy roads, several of them being our own wagons on their way to join us. We reached camp in the afternoon, built fires, and tried to dry ourselves out. Having no tents we were compelled to sleep again in the open air. But the wagons with our tents arrived the next morning and we made ourselves fairly comfortable.

Here at this camp the men devised a great sport to while away the dreary hours of the winter day. The snow was deep. What was more natural than that they should form themselves into companies and regiments, and with haversacks filled with snowballs march out and give battle to some of the neighboring regiments?

We planned a surprise attack on Toombs' Georgia brigade. The regiments of our brigade were put in line and in true battle formation moved forward to the attack, having previously thrown out skirmishers. We surprised the Georgians and took possession of their camp, and then they joined us and we went looking for new fields to conquer. We attacked and routed another brigade, after which we returned to our camp.

The prettiest of these battles (in which we were so often commanded by our own regular officers), so far as my experiment went, was one fought in March, 1864, while we were stationed in North Carolina, near Kinston.

In the early part of that month we had a delightful snow. In company with Surgeon Harold Snowden of our regiment I was engaged in trapping snow-birds when we heard music from a band coming up the road from the direction of the camp of General Hoke's North Carolina troops.

It proved to be Hoke's brigade, with the general and his staff riding at its head. When the troops came opposite to the place where our brigade was camped he halted his command and formed line of battle. I went over to see what it was all about and found General Hoke making them patriotic address, telling them of the invasion of their soil by the rascally Virginians and calling them to rally and drive the invaders out.

I was standing near the general, and I asked him if he did not intend to give us a chance to get ready. He said he would, and I turned and ran as fast as I could back to our camp, which was about three hundred yards away, calling out that Hoke's brigade was going to drive us from our camp. The alarm spread, the long roll was beat, and the Fifteenth, Seventeenth, and Thirtieth Regiments, which were camped together, began to form. But before we could do so the North Carolinians were upon us.

There was a rail fence just in front of our camp and the boys of our small command rallied behind it and held the attackers in check. But it was only for a few moments. They overpowered us and drove us through our camp into a swamp just in our rear, and those of us who could not escape either to the right or the left were forced into the swamp. Captain Fowle of my company and I went in over knee-deep.

While we were in this predicament we heard a joyful shout away down on our right from the direction of the camp of the Twenty-ninth Regiment of our brigade. They had received word of the attack and had formed almost to a man and were coming to our assistance at a double quick.

It was a real flank attack. The tide of battle was turned, and we rallied and drove them back through the camp. We captured several of General Hoke's staff officers and many of his men and one flag, and drove them in an opposite direction from their camp for several miles. It was reported that some of them did not get back to their camp until late in the night.

These contests were very exciting and needless to say, the men found a great measure of enjoyment in them.

CHAPTER XVI

MARCHING AND COUNTERMARCHING

WE remained in the neighborhood of Guinea Station until February 15, when we were ordered to move. Marching in the direction of Richmond, we arrived at Hanover Junction on the 16th and remained there all night. Details were made and sent back to assist in getting the wagons out of the mud.

An amusing incident which comes to my mind as I recall these marches happened one rainy day while Dr. M. M. Lewis was still our regimental surgeon. It was late in the day and we were about going into bivouac when a report came that a member of Company D had fallen, a mile or two back, and had broken his leg. The doctor hurried back and found that a member of the company had indeed met with that misfortune - but the leg was a wooden one! It belonged to a soldier who had lost his leg early in the war and had returned to duty when he recovered. You can imagine what the doctor said when he found out the nature of the injury.

The morning of the 17th was ushered in by a heavy snowstorm which continued until about 10 o'clock, when the snow turned to rain. Through this bad weather the men marched on until they arrived at a spot about ten miles from Richmond, when they went into bivouac wet and cold. The rain continued through the entire night and the following day but we resumed our march and at about 2 o'clock went into camp only a short distance from the city.

On the next day, the 19th, we passed through Richmond, marching in column of companies with our brigade the rear of the division. The streets were crowded with ladies and children to see us go through the city. The citizens treated us nicely, distributing food freely to the troops. We entered by the Brook Pike, marched down Broad Street to Ninth, down Ninth to Main, thence to Mayo's Bridge and across to Manchester and through it, and went into bivouac about two miles from the town. We remained here only overnight and then went on to Chester Station, about halfway between Richmond and Petersburg, where we stayed about ten days.

On our first night at Chester we were greeted by a heavy snowstorm which lasted for many hours, completely burying out of sight the entire division while it slept. We left this camp on March 1 and marched to and through Petersburg, going into camp about three miles below the city on the City Point road.

This march was a very severe one. The roads were in such a dreadful condition that the wagon trains did not arrive until the following day, although the distance was short. Our three-weeks' stay here was quietly spent, drills being resumed in spite of the fact that the weather continued extremely cold. Another heavy snowstorm set in on the evening of the 19th and the snow kept falling all night, all day and night of the 20th, and until the morning of the 21st, when it turned into a drizzling rain. There were fourteen or fifteen inches of snow on the ground.

At 1 o'clock on the morning of March 23 we received orders to move at daybreak. The regiment marched all day through the snow and slush, going into bivouac just before dark. The men immediately went to work to clear away the snow, collect wood, and gather branches of cedar and pine to spread upon the ground to sleep upon. A very disagreeable march brought us on the 25th to an encampment on swampy ground near Ivor Station on the Petersburg and Norfolk Railroad, where we remained until the 31st, when our regiment moved about four miles to Tucker Swamp Church, where we made camp in a very pretty piece of woods and settled down to regular camp life. Drills were resumed and regular picket duty by companies was done, the pickets being stationed on the Blackwater River. Our little force was called by the boys "The Army of the Blackwater." It consisted of the Seventeenth Virginia Regiment, Colonel Baker's Third North Carolina Cavalry, and a battery of artillery, and was under the command of Colonel Herbert.

At one of our camps during this period the following "General Order No. 46," signed by General R. E. Lee, was read to us:

"In obedience to the proclamation of the President of the Confederate States setting aside the 27th day of March as a day of fasting and prayer for the nation, all duties will be suspended on that day in the Army of Northern Virginia except such as are necessary for its safety and subsistence. Religious services appropriate to the occasion will be performed by the chaplains of their respective regiments.

"Soldiers! No portion of our people have greater cause to be thankful to Almighty God than yourselves. He has preserved your lives amid countless dangers. He has been with you in all your trials. He has given you fortitude under hardships and courage in the shock of battle.

"He has cheered you by the example and by the deed of your martyred comrades. He has enabled you to defend your country successfully against the assaults of a powerful oppressor.

"Devoutly thankful for His signal mercies, let us bow before the Lord of Hosts, and join our hearts with millions in our land in prayer that He will continue His merciful protection over our cause; that He will scatter our enemies, and set at naught their evil designs; and that He will graciously restore to our beloved country the blessings of peace and security."

While we were encamped here at Tucker Swamp Church the Twenty-ninth Virginia Regiment was attached to our brigade. It was a large and fine regiment but poorly officered, and on April 6 Colonel Arthur Herbert was assigned to command it temporarily. This put Major Simpson in command of the Seventeenth.

On April 9 we left this place and marched to Suffolk, where our command under Longstreet, laid siege to that town. Our regiment was separated from the others of the brigade and stationed on a narrow neck of land on the Dismal Swamp. Just before daybreak on the 15th, while we were still asleep, we were attacked by an enemy force consisting of the Hawkins Zouaves, the New York Mounted Rifles, and a battery of artillery. They forced us back across the swamp but our men then took position, made a stand, and succeeded in turning the tables on the enemy, compelling them to retire and recovering our lost ground.

Our command had about two hundred men in this fight. We had three wounded, and we lost four by capture. The wounded were T. B. Saunders and 0. F. Hoffman of Company K and Charles 0. Sipple of Company E.

On the next day the enemy attacked us again and by a cavalry charge succeeded in breaking our line, but with the assistance of the Fifteenth and Thirtieth Regiments of our brigade we managed to disperse them. On the 17th the Twenty-ninth Virginia was attacked but the charge was repulsed and the enemy driven back some distance. It was reported through the camp that the Twenty-ninth was so pleased with our colonel after this little fight that it asked to have him permanently assigned to it.

While we were here on this line, which extended from Dismal Swamp to the Nansemond River, General Pickett asked Captain Fowle of my company to send him a reliable man for scout duty within the enemy's lines. The company was then on duty at the outer picket line. The captain sent Sergeant J. P. Jordan, a man of unquestionable coolness and bravery who had been successful on several previous occasions of this kind. His instructions from the general were to enter the lines of the enemy and ascertain, if possible, the strength and situation of their camps and works.

Jordan selected three others to accompany him and they successfully accomplished their mission. General Pickett was so well pleased with their work that he issued a special order to be read on dress parade before the regiments and battalions of the division, praising them highly. "These gallant soldiers," he said in the order, "being sent by their commanding officers, when on picket duty on the New Somerton Road immediately in front of Suffolk, alone and unsustained pierced the enemy's line of skirmishers, penetrated to within a few yards of his main line of battle, gained valuable information, and returned, bringing with them four prisoners and all their arms and equipment."

Sergeant Jordan and one of the three men he took with him in this "act of gallant, chivalric daring," as General Pickett termed it, were members of Company H, the second man being Private J. T. Mills. The other two were members of Company F of the Thirtieth Virginia.

We remained in the neighborhood of Suffolk until May 3 when we withdrew, and crossing the Blackwater marched toward Petersburg, reaching there on the 8th. The next day we marched towards Richmond, arriving in the city that night. On the 16th we left the neighborhood of Richmond and marched to Hanover Junction, reaching there about noon on the 17th. There we went into regular camp and resumed drills.

While we were in Richmond we learned of the death of Stonewall Jackson, who died on May 10. His body was brought to

Richmond, where it lay in state in the Capitol building until the 13th when it was conveyed to Lexington, Va., for burial. General Corse of our brigade was one of the pallbearers.

Before we entered Richmond on this march I was detailed by General Corse to go to the city ahead of the brigade and deliver an important message. He supplied me with a horse and instructed me to deliver the message, receive an answer, and meet the command on a certain road on the other side of the city. He told me to be sure to return and report before daylight. This I came very near not doing.

It was early in the evening but very dark when I started. I delivered the message and received the answer without special incident, but as I was riding down Broad Street on my return journey, some time after midnight, I was halted by a mounted guard who had orders to scour the city in search of horses. In spite of my protest that I belonged to the regular army and was in the city under special orders the officer in charge would not release my horse which, incidentally, belonged to the general.

I was taken to Bacon Quarter Branch where the government stables were located. When I gave my name I was told that another soldier of the same name had just arrived. I asked to see him and was shown to his quarters. To my great delight he proved to be my father, who had come to the city in his capacity of forage master in Jackson's army to report to the post quartermaster, Major George Johnson (an Alexandrian).

I told father the circumstances of my being in Richmond and of my detention by the guard and told him also that I was to report to the general before daylight. He immediately went to Major Johnson, roused him from his sleep, and explained the matter to him, and the officer gave me an order for the release of my horse and another saying that I was not to be disturbed in leaving the city. After getting something to eat I left to rejoin the regiment and by hard riding arrived about daylight, tired and sleepy but on time.

At Hanover Junction we held the first elections for state officers. During the canvass we were highly entertained with speeches from the various candidates, and the excitement at times ran high.

Our assistant surgeon, Dr. Harold Snowden, was a candidate for the House of Delegates, opposing the incumbent, Mr. William G. Cazenove. When Mr. Cazenove came to the camp to make his canvass the Alexandrians of the regiment turned out and called on the doctor (whom they almost idolized) to make a speech. We arranged some boxes for him to stand upon and the speech and meeting were a great success. At the ensuing election Dr. Snowden was victorious.

On May 26, 1863, orders were read on dress parade to the effect that commanders of regiments and brigades should not mention in their reports of battles the number of men carried into action. This was evidently for the purpose of keeping that information from the enemy.

Our regiment on June 2 was ordered to guard a wagon train which was to go down into King and Queen County, for supplies. We had reports from some citizens that the enemy was advancing from below and had burned several dwellings and barns, but we learned that it was only a scouting party. The next morning we marched back to Newtown to await the rest of our brigade and on the day following, after uniting with it, we started for Hanover Junction. But we were soon halted by reports brought in by mounted citizens that the enemy were landing from boats and destroying property in the lower part of the county.

Our regiment under Colonel Herbert was ordered back and when beyond the village was formed in line of battle. My company was ordered out in advance on picket duty. We could see clouds of smoke away off in the distance but we saw nothing of the enemy and soon we rejoined our command. We moved off in the direction of Culpeper but found ourselves presently at a place called Taylorsville, a village of three or four houses on the l not far from Hanover Junction. We were given the duty of guarding the railroad bridge over that stream. While we were here a new chaplain, the Rev. Robert Baker of the Protestant Episcopal Church, was assigned to us.

We had a good time at this camp. It was nicely located and we had lots of bathing and fishing and no drilling. But such good fortune was not to last any great length of time. On the morning of June 8 we were relieved by some North Carolina troops and rejoined our division, which was then near Culpeper. On the plains near that place I witnessed what was considered one of the most magnificent sights of the war, the passing of Stuart's entire cavalry command of about 8,000 in review before General Lee.

While the Army of Northern Virginia started off on the Gettysburg campaign Corse's brigade of Pickett's division was still in camp at this place. It was perhaps the strongest in numbers of all the brigades in their division. We were ordered to remain behind for the purpose of keeping open communications in Virginia and protecting the line of railroads from Richmond to Gordonsville, and the city of Richmond itself, from raiding parties of the enemy. It was a tiresome duty and it kept our brigade constantly on the move.

On June 25 we were ordered to Gordonsville. On the night of the 28th we were hurriedly put on cars and rushed to Richmond. Arriving there at daybreak we stacked arms on the sidewalk, awaiting further orders. They soon came and we were sent out about three miles from the city, only to be put on the cars again on the following night and after a tiresome ride cheered by rations of hard tack and bacon landed again at Gordonsville.

That night while in bivouac we were surprised by the appearance among us of G. William Ramsay, who at beginning of the war the had been considered too young to enlist. He had left Alexandria in an endeavor to make his way through the lines of the enemy to join us and after several thrilling adventures had succeeded.

I remember well when he made his appearance. It was just about twilight and Ed Roxbury of my company, who had a sweet voice, was singing to us as we sat around our campfire, accompanying himself on a guitar that he had borrowed from a nearby farmhouse. He sang something about "A lover returned from the war, his spirit so light and so gay." Ed survived the war but shortly after its close died in Washington. Will Ramsay that night enlisted in the Alexandria Riflemen.

We remained here until July 8 when we broke camp and marched to the Valley, starting off in a drenching rain. After going about twenty miles we camped near Madison Court House. The next day found us near Milan's Gap in the Blue Ridge Mountains, which we crossed, and we then went into camp near Luray. After fording the Shenandoah River we arrived on July 13 at Winchester, where we learned the particulars of the Gettysburg campaign and learned also that our army was returning to Virginia. Our day's march was gladdened by the sight of the prisoners our army had taken at Gettysburg. They numbered nearly 5,000 and were on their way under heavy guard to Staunton.

Here also we heard of the gallant part which our division (Pickett's) had taken in the charge at Gettysburg. In connection with this charge I would like to give the following extract from a letter dated July 23 which General Pickett wrote to the lady who afterwards became his wife:

"If the charge made by my gallant Virginians on the fatal third of July had been supported, or even if my other two brigades, Jenkins' and Corse's, had been with me, we would now, I believe, have been in Washington and the war practically over."

After remaining at Winchester several days our brigade received orders to precede the army down the Valley as the advance. We started on the morning of July 20 towards Front Royal and halted for the night at the village of Cedarville, five miles from that town. On resuming our march the next morning we had to ford the Shenandoah, a difficult feat as the stream was swollen and the current rapid. To keep from being washed away and drowned the men joined hands and helped each other in crossing. I crossed by holding on to a horse's tail. But we all managed to reach the other bank in safety and we proceeded on our way to Front Royal.

CHAPTER XVII

A CLOSE CALL FOR THE SEVENTEENTH

THE stage was now set for one of the most thrilling adventures the Seventeenth Virginia was to experience in its whole career. For half a day it fought an engagement, entirely alone, in which it was greatly outnumbered and partially surrounded by the enemy but in which it successfully defended a mountain pass until relieved by a brigade from the main army. By the chances of war I happened to be the agency through which the relief was brought in time.

As Lee's army slowly defiled southward down the Shenandoah Valley behind the mountain wall of the Blue Ridge the enemy rightly surmised that the Valley pike would be strewn with its long trains, and pushed forward their cavalry into all the gaps from Ashby's to Thornton's, watching for a chance to break through and attack. Our brigade, it seems, was sent forward to guard these passes and defend the flanks of the army.

We arrived at Front Royal on the morning of July 21. The weather was scorching hot. The Seventeenth Virginia Regiment, under the command of Major Simpson, was detached from the brigade and ordered to move up into the mountain gap through which the Manassas Gap railroad passes. (Our colonel, Arthur Herbert, had been detailed some time before to bring into a state of discipline a refractory regiment which had shaved the tail of its colonel's horse and was in open hostility towards him. Colonel Herbert was then in Front Royal on his way to rejoin us.)

The regiment took up its line of march on up the dusty road and before noon reached a place near the center of the pass. We filed into the woods on the right of the road and stacked our arms parallel with the road and about twenty yards from it. Up to this time everything had looked quiet and peaceful and the men, little expecting the enemy to make his appearance so early, were soon busy in the adjoining fields gathering blackberries, which grew in profusion there. Three companies (mere remnants of companies) had been sent out to do picket duty over the mountain.

While the bulk of the men were thus busily engaged in enjoying themselves I strolled up the road in the direction of our pickets. Mason Washington of Company K was with me. We had gone about three hundred yards when we were joined by our surgeon, Dr. J. W. Leftwich, on horseback. The doctor had dismounted and we were standing talking when Adjutant W. W. Zimmerman, who had gone out to post the pickets, came riding furiously towards us, shouting as he hurried on:

"To arms! Fall in! The enemy is coming!"

He rode rapidly by us and on to the regiment. Then followed a helter-skelter race by the men from the fields in an effort to get their positions in the ranks. They had hardly succeeded in doing so before the advance of the enemy's cavalry, who had already captured most of our pickets, came galloping in sight from a cross road about seventy-five yards from where we were standing.

Washington saw them first and shouted, "Here they are!" He and the surgeon leaped the fence and ran down and through the woods to the regiment, the surgeon calling to me to mount his horse and ride in to Front Royal and give the alarm. I mounted and started down the road in the direction of the command.

In the meantime the enemy's advance, ten in number, were coming on at full speed. They shouted to me, "Halt, there, and surrender!" and immediately began firing. To an onlooker the spectacle of the chase would no doubt have been most diverting. But to me riding there alone, the sole object for the enemy to shoot at, it was anything in the world but enjoyable.

They had not yet discovered the position of the regiment. I rode down and passed across its front. The regiment had succeeded in forming near the edge of the woods, about twenty yards from the road. Some of the boys shouted at me as I went by, "Go it, Warfield, go it!" The chase led the enemy within this close range and when they were directly in front of the regiment a volley from more than fifty rifles rendered the ten horses riderless. Our officers had called to the troops to spare the horses but get the men and that is what they did. Only one horse was wounded and that but slightly. The entire advance of Federals was killed outright, none wounded. They proved to be members of the First U. S. Regular Cavalry, which with the Second and Fifth Regulars composed the cavalry brigade of General Merritt. It outnumbered many times our little force of about 225 men.

I continued into Front Royal and was fired on again before reaching the town. Some of the enemy had succeeded in getting in the rear of our regiment and were trying to get possession of the road I was then on. They captured it before I had reached Front Royal.

I knew that a number of our officers were being entertained at the house of a member of Company B, and I hastened there and rapped loudly on the door. It was opened by Mr. M. M. Lewis, chief surgeon of Pickett's division. Here I found Colonel Herbert and five or six officers of Pickett's staff, among them Captain E. R. Baird. I hurriedly told them all that had occurred and was still occurring up in the mountain and the state of affairs between the town and the regiment.

Captain Baird immediately pressed me into service, ordering me to proceed in the direction of Winchester and keep going until I met General Pickett, who was coming this way with the remnants of his division acting as the advance of the main army. I of course obeyed, starting off bareheaded (I had lost my hat in the meantime), and presently reached the Shenandoah River just above the town. The water was deep and was running rapidly and the crossing was somewhat risky. I hesitated but a moment. Realizing the importance of my errand I forced my horse into the water and succeeded in reaching the opposite side safely and then struck out rapidly towards Winchester. I had not gone far before I met the advance of the troops with General Pickett riding at the head of the column.

I repeated my story to the general, talking loudly enough so that the boys who had crowded up to the front at sight of my rapid approach could hear everything. The general questioned me about the position of the regiment and the enemy, winding up with the inquiry, "Where in the devil is our cavalry?" I told him we had none with us. Thinking my work done I was about to fall in with his mounted men at the rear when he turned to Major Joseph C. Cabell of the Thirty-eighth Virginia who was in command of what was left of Armisted's brigade and directed him to hasten to the relief of our regiment. (Major Cabell, afterwards Colonel Cabell, was killed at the Battle of Drewry's Bluff, May 16, 1864.) Then turning to me he ordered me to show the troops the way in.

On learning that the Seventeenth Virginia was in a tight place and that they were being sent to its relief the men of the brigade started off at rapid gait, cheering as they went. They lost no time in reaching and fording the river and were soon on their way to Front Royal where they were joined by Captain Baird. Marching at route step they were hurried up into the Gap, with Major Cabell at their head. I rode by the Major's side.

We had gone but a short distance when I had the nerve to volunteer the suggestion that I thought we had gone far enough on the road for safety. This suggestion on my part, if not a violation of regulations, was at least a breach of military etiquette. But I knew that I was acting as a guide by order and that I had better knowledge of the situation than anyone else there. So I made bold to speak although fearing a rebuke for doing so.

But I did not know my commander. I shall never forget the look on his face. It was a kindly look - he was probably amused at my nerve in advising my commander on the field what to do. But he evidently thought well of the advice for he said, "If you think so I will halt right here." He immediately halted his command advanced his skirmishers, who had not gone more than two hundred yards before they became hotly engaged with the skirmishers of the enemy. In a few minutes the entire force was engaged. The men succeeded in driving the Union forces before them and they were soon united with the Seventeenth Virginia. Colonel Herbert, who had reached his regiment before our arrival, now assumed command of the entire force as he was the ranking officer.

The Seventeenth had put up a good fight previous to the arrival of the reinforcements which was not until late in the afternoon. It had more than held the enemy in check. Besides repulsing all their advances it had made several successful charges itself, driving them each time. But the boys of the regiment said it was a glorious sight when the red battle-flag of Cabell and his men came up across the fields to their relief, driving the enemy before them.

Lieutenant Slaughter of Company K, writing later of the arrival of these reinforcements, described the experience of the command in these words:

"Slowly the sun went up the eastern heavens, slowly he approached the meridian, slowly he descended towards the west and seemed for hours to stand still in the sky. The enemy every moment were growing stronger and charged again and again. The little regiment suffered from hunger and thirst, heat and smoke, but stood firm across the path. And no help came, and still the fight went on until the declining sun almost touched the distant mountain tops. And then in the distance, oh, joyful sound! - the beating of a drum is heard and oh, glorious sight! - the battle-flag of the Confederacy is seen, and under its fold come the long gray line of veterans to the rescue."

The only mention of this important day's work, so far as I have been able to learn, is in the reports of General Longstreet and General Merritt. From Longstreet's report, dated at Culpeper Court House, July 27, 1863, I quote as follows:

"On the night of the 20th reached Millwood. The Shenandoah was found to be past fording. On the following day, July 21, the river still past fording, the laying of our bridges was begun.

"General Corse, who had hurried forward with his brigade, had succeeded in crossing the stream, detaching a regiment to Manassas Gap. He marched his main force to Chester Gap and succeeded in getting possession of the latter a few moments before the enemy appeared.

"The enemy was in possession of the east end of Manassas Gap. But Colonel Arthur Herbert secured a strong position with the regiment, from which he held the enemy in check. Reinforcements were sent to Colonel Herbert, when he drove back the enemy and secured and secured as much of the Gap as was desirable."

General Merritt's report was dated at Manassas Gap, "July 21, 1863, evening of the fight, 9 p.m." and was as follows:

"We have had two small fights with the enemy at the west end of the Gap, the first in which the First Cavalry was engaged in attempting to penetrate to Front Royal, the second in which the First, Second, and Fifth were engaged for the same object. I found the enemy in force at the west end of the Gap.

"I can learn nothing further in regard to Lee's army, more than what I have already reported. The only prisoners taken are all from the

Seventeenth Virginia Regiment Infantry and number about twenty, including four commissioned officers. The regiment is about 600 strong, which of itself in this country is enough to hold my entire brigade in check as I can not use my artillery to advantage.

"The wounds inflicted on the men of my brigade are very severe and the arms captured from the enemy are the Springfield rifle. Longstreet is at Front Royal and it is said has sent out a force this way and towards Chester Gap. I at first thought they had only one regiment in my front but am now convinced that Hoover's brigade of Corse's division is this side of Front Royal. The fact that we have captured prisoners from only one regiment is attributed to this regiment being on picket duty. I will feel them again in the morning."

The general was in error on several counts. There was no such brigade as Hoover's and no such division as Corse's in Lee's army. During the day and until nearly dark he was confronted by only about 225 men of the Seventeenth Virginia Regiment. The reinforcements under Cabell numbered only 600 men. Neither did the general make the slightest attempt to feel us out in the morning.

The command remained all night in front of the enemy, occasionally exchanging shots which did little damage. But there was no need for the Seventeenth to do more here at Manassas Gap. It had saved the artillery and trains of the Confederate army that were passing, and there is no telling what futher mischief General Merritt might have done with his large force if he had struck the retreating line, for we had no cavalry to head him of at any point.

In this fight the regiment had its color-bearers shot down three times. One of them, Robert Buchanan of my company, received his death wound. He had seized the colors after they had fallen the first time and carried them forward, waving them in front of the regiment. But he went only a few yards before he fell.

This General Merritt is the same commander who later in the war received and carried out the folllowing order from General Phil Sheridan while in the Valley of Virginia:

"Headquarters Middle Military Division,
Harrisburg, Va., September 20, 1864.

"Brigadier General W. Merritt, commanding First Cavalry Division: Destroy all mills, all grain and forage. You can drive off or kill all stock and otherwise carry out the instructions of Lt.-Gen'l Grant, an extract of which is sent you, and which means, 'Leave the Valley a barren waste.'

"Jas. W. Forsythe, Lt. Colonel and Chief
of Staff to Major General Sheridan."

CHAPTER XVIII

GUARD DUTY IN THREE STATES

WE passed through the Gap on July 22 and marched to Culpeper Court House, where we remained until August 3. Then we moved to the neighborhood of Rapidan Station for a five weeks' stay, allowing the regiment to rest and recruit.

A great religious revival occurred at about this time. The reader must not suppose that the spiritual comforts of the soldiers were neglected. Cut off as they were from all the happy influences of home and loved ones, subjected to severe temptations, often having no day of sacred rest, and in contact only with their fellow comrades-in-arms, the men bore all their hardships with a truly wonderful patience. Prayer meetings were held whenever opportunities occurred and ministers of different denominations frequently preached to the men in camp.

The prayer meetings were conducted by the officers of the regiment and were well attended. The men joined in the prayers and their voices in the singing would ring out loud and clear in the quiet nights.

From the camp at Rapidan Station we moved through Gordonsville and Louisa Court House to Richmond, where after a day's stop we took the cars for Petersburg, and on the next day our brigade was sent by rail to Lynchburg and thence to Zillicoffer, Tennessee. Here we had a very pleasant time. Food was plentiful and the fruit was of the finest quality.

One day a party of us went over the mountain to visit some farm houses where we could buy apple butter. We stopped at one house and found on the premises a fine cider press with apples in abundance ready to be put in the mill. We went to work to make cider for our party and were soon having a fine time of it. But hardly was the work well under way when the bullets began zipping around us. We were being fired upon by the skirmishers of an advancing cavalry force. We were taken completely by surprise, as we had no idea that any of the enemy were near us. We left the place in a hurry without getting any apple butter and we left behind a quantity of nice cider. On September 20, three days after our arrival, we had a slight skirmish with this body of cavalry on the mountain top and easily repulsed them.

We remained in Tennessee until the end of the month and then we were again put on the cars and headed for Virginia, going first to Lynchburg and then, a few days later, to Ivor Station on the Petersburg and Norfolk Railroad. We were told that we would likely spend the winter there and we soon made ourselves comfortable.

The camp was regularly laid out. Most of the men built log huts in which to live instead of tents. Our mess, consisting of "Wash" Milburn, Thomas Chauncey, and myself, had one of the finest houses in the camp.

Here I had my first experience at hog-killing. By exercising a great deal of patience and perseverance we had succeeded in enticing a hog into our quarters, aided by a handful or two of shelled corn. We closed the door and proceeded to dispose of his pigship. All we had to do it with was an ax and we struck many blows, several of which missed their mark, before the poor animal, literally hacked to pieces, gave up the ghost. We had no means for scalding and scraping it and we had to content ourselves with skinning it. We found ourselves well fixed for meat for several days. These hogs were not the property of anyone, simply running wild. But it would not have mattered to us if they had been. We were hungry.

While we were in these quarters Milburn, who had seen one of his country comrades make a very nice dish out of persimmons, obtained the recipe and cooked up a quantity of them for himself. But after he had boiled them for three or four hours he had to give up. There was nothing palatable about the mess. However, he determined that his labor should not go for nothing and threw in one of his old cotton shirts. It was dyed a very pretty brown and was the envy and admiration of all who saw it.

Food was quite plentiful here, as the country people were willing to sell their produce to the soldiers. So we enjoyed our stay at Ivor and regretted when the time came to move.

Speaking of food I must tell of one little happening that enlivened our camp life here. The government required that a tythe, or one-tenth, of certain farm products should be delivered to it for the maintenance of the army. While we were here the farmers of Southampton and adjoining counties brought in a large quantity of beans and piled them up on the station platform ready to be forwarded by the collectors to Petersburg the next day.

A guard was placed over the pile of bags - he was Private Rudd of Company E. He perched himself on top of the high pile of bags, judging that he could see from that vantage point whatever was going on all around him. He was right about that, but he did not reckon on what might be going on out of sight underneath him until he felt that the pile of beans on which he sat was slowly and quietly settling down under him. It seems that a number of his comrades had crawled under the platform and had pushed up their bayonets through the broad cracks of the platform and ripped the bags, and the beans were gradually pouring down through the cracks and into the bags which the boys had brought for the purpose of holding them.

Our stay here was enlivened by an occasional scout in the direction of the enemy, with now and then an exchange of shots in which we always came off best. It was also varied by frequent visits to Petersburg, as passes for twenty-four or forty-eight hours could be easily obtained from Colonel Herbert. Two of our boys once made good use of this privilege for business purposes. One of them was a composer of quite a number of camp songs and the other was suffering from some trouble with his eye which looked much worse than it really was. The eyes of this second man were bandaged, with just enough of the bad eye showing to excite sympathy, and then he was led about the streets by his composer-companion while he sold the songs, printed on slips. They did quite a lively business for a few days until the colonel stopped their game.

A number of refugees from Norfolk came into our camp at Ivor, forced out by the persecutions of the enemy. They consisted entirely of women and children. At times they would have to remain one or two nights in our camp as the trains from Petersburg ran down here only twice a week. Our boys cheerfully surrendered their quarters to them and made the time as pleasant as possible for them with such entertainment as could be provided.

Notwithstanding we were compelled to attend regimental drills every day, the officers and men found ample time for pleasure. Among other things the officers held a tournament which passed off successfully. It was a test of riding skill, the officer attempting to pierce a small ring with a lance while riding at full speed. The successful knight was privileged to crown the queen of love and beauty at the ball held that evening in the railroad station, to which the ladies of the neighborhood were invited and which was well attended by them. Of course the boys had to have their tournament, too. They held it that night by moonlight, riding the horses from the wagon yard and using fence rails for lances and barrel hoops for rings.

One Morning we were ordered to fall in without arms, and the order caused a little stir of curiosity among the boys as to the reason. They soon found out. The colonel stated that the gentleman who was with him had made a complaint that a squad claiming to be a provost guard and under a lieutenant had called at his house the night before in search of liquor. They found some in the basement and emptied it into a washtub and carried it off. The farmer said he could identify the lieutenant and that was the reason for the call of the regiment.

He was led slowly down the line but he failed to identify the guilty man. That man nevertheless was in the line and had looked the farmer full in the face as he passed by. The guilty one was a sergent who had borrowed a lieutenant's jacket and sword. A few days later, when the colonel found out whose uniform had been used, the lieutenant to whom it belonged was reduced to the ranks. When this bogus guard had reached the camp the night before with their capture they had filled all the canteens they could borrow from the boys. Mine was among the number although I had not known what it was to be used for until the farmer made his complaint. The washtub after being emptied had been broken up and burned.

On January 23 we bade farewell to our quarters at Ivor. The many pleasant hours we spent there are well remembered by the boys of the old Seventeenth. We took train for Petersburg, remained there a few days, and on the 28th departed for Kinston, North Carolina, where we arrived two days later. On the same evening we began a march to Newbern, on which place we started to make an attack.

138

This march was the longest forced march ever made by the regiment. It was also probably the most trying one. We had several small streams to cross, over which we had to pass one at a time. The roads were so deep in sand that many of the men removed their shoes and marched barefooted. The distance of fifty-three miles was made in about twenty-seven hours - remarkable time, considering the conditions. The command consisted of a regiment of cavalry, a battery of artillery, and our regiment, all under the command of Colonel James Dearing. The other regiment of our brigade, under General Corse, were on the other side of the Neuse River.

The attack was not made, for the reason given in the following extract from General Pickett's report to the adjutant general:

"In the attack on Newbern, the enemy was reinforcing heavily by railroad and trying to rake our lines with guns on a steam ironclad. They attempted to turn our right flank with these reinforcements. I threw Corse's command forward to drive them in, which he did handsomely."

We returned to Kinston, arriving there on February 5, but were ordered the next day to Goldsboro, North Carolina, and from there on the 24th to Lexington in the same state. We were sent to Lexington to stop a local disturbance but the report was greatly exaggerated and we found everything quiet on our arrival. The trip was a pleasant one and we were hospitably entertained by the citizens.

As this section of country was not in the war zone the people had seen no soldiers of either army. At their request Colonel Herbert ordered both the Fifteenth (which had accompanied us) and the Seventeenth to form, and we put on a drill and dress parade for the entertainment of the citizens. We then returned to Goldsboro.

Early in February Major General Pickett had been assigned to the command of the Department of North Carolina and Virginia, with headquarters in Petersburg. Surgeon M. M. Lewis, who was surgeon of the Seventeenth Virginia at the beginning of the war and later brigade surgeon of Longstreet's Brigade, was now chief surgeon of Pickett's division. He asked for my appointment as division hospital steward but the request was not granted because of the great desire of our regimental commander to keep the roll of Company H (his old company) from

139

falling below the minimum number of twenty-eight men, thereby opening it to conscripts. I knew nothing of the matter until another man had been appointed. I thus lost an opportunity to ride with Pickett and his staff, wear a "biled shirt", and have a much easier time.

On a previous occasion I had been asked if I would accept the position of hospital steward, in which I would have been directly under the orders of the Secretary of War. The intention was to assign me to an artillery battalion that was about to be transferred to North Carolina. I did not want the appointment, as it would take me away from my companions and put me among strangers. So I declined.

March 7 found us back in Kinston where we went into camp on the banks of the Neuse River. On our arrival in the town we staked our arms on the sidewalk and lay down to sleep alongside of our guns. During the night a heavy rain fell. With one other soldier I found shelter by crawling under a doorstep, where we kept ourselves comparatively dry.

The day after our arrival I borrowed a bag from one of our wagon drivers and went out to gather some cresses that grew abundantly along the banks of a nearby stream. I filled the bag and had enough for more than a dozen men, but I had no meat or even salt to put with them. The dish was about to prove very unpalatable when the situation was happily saved by the colonel, who happened to come up while I was cooking my cresses. He stopped to talk a while and found that I had no meat. He was in almost the same fix as myself. He was having visitors from the town to lunch with him and he had some bacon but nothing to cook with it. He suggested that he should put it in with my cresses and we would divide at the finish. I gladly accepted and we both profited by the deal.

On April 1 we were ordered out to witness the execution of a conscript member of Company G, who had been tried for desertion by a court-martial at Petersburg and sentenced to be shot.

On May 3 we were ordered back for another attack on Newbern, but after we had arrived at that town and had taken our places in line of battle the attack was called off. The occasion was the receipt of important news front Virginia. General Grant had commenced his movements in front of General Lee and the Battle of the Wilderness was on. We were ordered back to Kinston in a hurry, in the darkness. In order to deceive the enemy I with a number of others was detailed to remain until about midnight to keep the camp fires burning. At about that hour we left and being in light marching order soon overtook the regiment.

CHAPTER XIX

FIGHTING ON SHORT RATIONS

EXTRA rations were issued and we started for Virginia. We arrived at Petersburg on the afternoon of May 12, much to the relief of the citizens as Butler and his command were in front of the place. We found on our arrival that the city's forces were few in number and entirely too small to cope with the enemy and that they consisted mainly of local defense troops.

General Pickett successfully used a clever ruse to deceive the enemy. He ran empty trains slowly and noiselessly out of the city for a mile or two and then rushed them back with the usual loud noise, creating the impression that he was receiving heavy reinforcements.

The next day we were put on the cars of the Southside Railroad and carried to Brookville Junction. We had previously tried to reach Richmond by the pike but had met with resistance and had been forced to retrace our steps to Petersburg. At the junction we were transferred to the Danville road and run up to Flat Creek in Amelia County, where a large cavalry raiding party was endeavoring to reach and destroy the railroad and county bridges. On this run I was placed with a number of others on top of a box car next to the engine as we expected every moment to be attacked from the roadside by the enemy.

As soon as we arrived at the bridges we began to barricade. About daybreak next morning our pickets beyond the bridges were driven in by the advance of the enemy. Making use of their artillery and charging with dismounted cavalry they tried to get possession of the bridges and destroy them. But after several attempts had failed they retired, leaving a number of their dead behind. We followed, driving them toward Amelia Court House.

The enemy force proved to be a brigade of German cavalry with six pieces of artillery under the command of General Aaron V. Kautz, who stated in his report of the operations on the Richmond and Danville Railroad that "Colonel Spear and Major Jacobs with portions of their commands, were sent up the road to make a demonstration on Flat Creek Bridge while the rest of the command were engaged in destroying the

142

track, etc. Finding that Flat Creek Bridge was *strongly contested* the column was put in motion towards the south."

Many months later this fight at Flat Creek Bridge had a very pleasant little aftermath. The good people of Amelia did not forget the work of the Seventeenth Virginia in saving the bridges and on the Christmas following the boys were the recipients of an elegant dinner sent by the citizens of that vicinity as a token of their appreciation of our success.

We sent them a letter of thanks which was printed in one of the Richmond papers with the comment that "it comes from a regiment that from the 18th of July, 1861, to this day has signalized its courage on as many battlefields and won as proud a name as any that marches under the banners of our beloved Confederacy." The letter was as follows:

"Camp Seventeenth Virginia Infantry,
January 1, 1865.

"To the Citizens of Amelia County Va.: With much gratitude and pleasure we acknowledge the receipt of your liberal donation of a Christmas dinner through the Hands of Rev. Mr. Littleton, a donation all the more appreciated from its being unexpected.

"We accept it as a spontaneous overflow of kind sympathy for soldiers unknown to you, and whose only claim upon your notice was a simple act of duty. As refugees we appreciate the donation highly and still more the motive that prompted it.

"It adds another incentive to nerve us for coming trials and dangers in a cause so sacred and dear to us all, and we will ever look back upon it as a pleasant episode in our history as a regiment.

"May a kind Providence ever protect the homes and hearthstones of such friendly and sympathetic hearts. We send you our greetings for the New Year. May it be a happy and prosperous one, and may you ever have as willing hearts to defend you, in your need, as beat in the breasts of your friends -

"The Officers and Soldiers of the
Seventeenth Virginia Infantry."

On Sunday, May 15, 1864, we received orders which

143

transferred us to Manchester (opposite Richmond), where we took cars which carried the brigade to the neighborhood of Drewry's Bluff. There the command took position in line of battle. On the next day the Battle of Drewry's Bluff was fought, in which our brigade under General Corse drove the enemy in fine style from their entrenchments and pursued them for more than a mile. In the excitement of the charge the General shouted out to his men:

"Wade in, my bullies, wade in!"

Just previous to the commencement of this charge and while the general was passing down the rear of the line giving his instructions the men, who had had nothing to eat since the morning before, cried out "Bread! Bread!" The general told them they would have all they needed soon as they were to charge the enemy's works in a few minutes and they would find plenty to eat over there. This proved to be true and as we passed through the works it was amusing to see the men taking up the pursuit while holding their guns in one hand and munching crackers from the other.

The regiment directly in front of us was the One Hundredth New York. Our loss in this fight, killed and wounded, was thirty-one. Among the killed was Corporal John T. Mills of my company. With the help of a comrade I buried his body by the roadside, simply wrapped in his blanket.

Rations, which were so abundant in the first year of the war, gradually began to decline both in quality and in quantity and as the war progressed failure to issue any at all was no uncommon occurence in the Army of Northern Virginia. Even when the issue was made the soldier might be told that in lieu of meat he would get coffee, and that to the amount of seven grains per man per day, twenty-one grains being counted out for three days. Every old soldier will remember as a part of his experience that more than once he had to rely on the commissary of the enemy for his next meal.

Flour when issued was often inconvenient to handle and make into bread. One of the plans adopted when pans could not be had was to make a hole in the ground and spread over it an oil-cloth, the hollow in which served as a tray in which to work the dough. Then the dough was made into long strips, which were wound around a ramrod and held over the fire to be cooked.

During the latter months of the war the issuance of rations to the men was so uncertain that it was almost a mystery how they lived. The last issue of rations to our command at Appomattox prior to surrender was for two days and consisted of two ears of hard corn to a man, per day. This corn was taken from that intended for the horses.

It was after a battle that the Confederate soldier could eat his fill. Then when opportunity offered to plunder a deserted camp of the enemy or to get at their wagon trains frequently he could get ground roasted coffee enough to last him many days. Desiccated vegetables and all kinds of canned goods, beef ready cooked, and fancy crackers, astonished the stomach of the "boy in gray". Haversacks were filled to the uttermost, and loaded down with all he could carry he would plod on to join his comrades on the weary march.

Frequently to get bread we would grate the hard corn on the cob against an old piece of tin which had been perforated with nails. The meal obtained in this way was mixed with water, often with no salt, and made into a kind of cake, which constituted our rations for several days.

Often the corn meal issued to us contained much of the cob ground in with the grain. So bad did it become at times that an issue of hardtack, an article of food almost unknown to the present generation, was hailed with delight. Hardtack in the hands of an expert "Confed" (and they were all experts) was made very palatable when he could by any means get a little bacon grease. The cracker was soaked well and then fried in the grease. Such delicacies were known as "mucks" by the boys. He was considered a lucky chap who could get as much as the smallest piece of fat bacon to cook with his hardtack.

Then the scarcity of cooking utensils was a great drawback to us. For months at a time we had to get along with one frying pan to the company. The occasional quarrels by the claimants for the next turn in the use of that implement helped to break the monotony of camp life.

One of the camp jokes about this common frying pan was that after it was used by a mess it would be placed outside of the men's tent or shelter to be licked clean by the camp dog and thus made ready for use by the next mess.

We had such a dog for a while, a present to one of the members

145

of Company H by his sweetheart, who lived at a place called "the picket post" down in Southampton County, a place well known to all members of the Seventeenth Regiment. But poor "Sadler," after being with us for some months, met with an untimely death. He had his throat cut, by orders. The occasion was a secret night march in close proximity to the enemy and he was executed to prevent his persistent barking from giving the alarm.

That march, incidentally, was an eventful one and will never be forgotten by those participating in it. It occurred while Grant was moving into position around Richmond. We were told that the advance of both armies was making for the same position and on parallel routes. Officers were constantly riding up and down the lines, encouraging and urging the men to keep up and hurry on, telling them of the importance of the movement and enjoining the utmost silence. No loud talking was allowed, canteens and bayonet scabbards were so arranged as not to rattle or make a noise.

At one time a staff officer rode through our ranks telling us that General Lee was close behind on his way to the front and that we were to quietly open ranks for him to pass but that there must positively be no cheering. Then came an unforgettable sight - this silent body of men rushing on in the darkness of the night, opening ranks for their commander to pass, with no cheering but with every hat raised and waving. We gained the position and the enemy was compelled to move on.

Rations of meat, when issued to the men, were turned over to the company sergeant by the regimental commissary. After cutting it up into small pieces according to the number of men in the company, the sergeant would ask one of the men whose back was turned who should have the piece he was holding. This was continued until all was distributed. Crackers were counted out, so many to a man. Frequently a three days' ration was devoured at one meal, so small was the allowance.

When the campaign in northern Virginia began in May, 1864, the commanding general reported only two days' rations on hand in Richmond for the army. On June 23 he reported thirteen days' rations on hand and on December 5 rations for nine days. On December 14 he informed the President that the army was without meat.

Because of the high prices in Confederate money the civilian population shared to a certain extent in these privations. I have before me a menu of the Ballard Hotel, in Richmond, printed in 1864 while Mr. J. C. Taliaferro, late of Alexandria, was proprietor of that famous hostelry. The epicure of those days had to have a fortune if he desired to satisfy his cravings for seasonal delicacies. No article on the bill of fare was figured lower than one dollar and from that level the prices ranged upward to a maximum of twenty dollars, the cost of a spring chicken. A breakfast of coffee, bread, and bacon and eggs cost ten dollars, dinner at the lowest was fifty-seven dollars, and supper could not be had for less than seven dollars and a half, so that the guest of the Ballard Hotel found himself faced with a bill of not less than $74 per day. The bill of fare was as follows:

Ham and eggs	$ 5.00	Butter	$ 1.00
Ham and cabbage	5.00	Eggs, plain	3.00
Potatoes	5.00	Onions	4.00
Roast Beef	5.00	Chicken	20.00
Shad	5.00	Raw oysters	5.00
One-half dozen fried		Coffee or tea	3.00
oysters	7.00	Corn bread	3.00
Milk toast	3.00		

On the market apples were selling for $3 per dozen, tomatoes $1 each, onions $1 each, and potatoes $4 per quart. At the same time the soldier's pay was $16 per month, Confederate money.

One would imagine from the meagerness and uncertainty of his food supply that the Confederate soldier would have become dissatisfied and discouraged and would have developed a growling disposition, or that he might even have been ready and willing to desert at the first opportunity. But such was not the case. With all his suffering he remained cheerful, marching ever on to meet an enemy who was comfortably clad and well fed. The best evidence of this state of mind was his readiness to reenlist when his term of service was up.

At the beginning of our struggle in 1861 the Virginia troops were mustered in and sworn in for one year's service as state troops. Before the year was up we were transferred to the service of the Confederate States. At the close of the year's enlistment we were called to enlist for two years more and did so, and at the close of the three years we were asked to enlist for the duration of the war.

This final reenlistment, coming as it did when the men were so badly clothed and on such short rations, showed strikingly the zeal and determination of the Confederate soldier to see the struggle through to the end. In spite of all the adverse conditions General Lee was able to report that nearly every regiment in the Army of Northern Virginia had enlisted for the duration of the war.

My regiment had a conspicuous part in this action. One of the proud pages on its record is the following resolution adopted by the Virginia Legislature in its 1864 session:

"Resolved, that the thanks of the General Assembly of Virginia are due and are hereby tendered to Lieutenant Colonel Arthur Herbert, of the Seventeenth Regiment of Virginia Infantry, Corse's brigade, Pickett's division, and the gallant troops under his command, for the determination they have shown to uphold and defend the independence of Virginia and the Confederate states, as is evidenced by their action on Monday the 15th instant, on which they *re-enlisted for the war.*"

This spirit and action were general throughout the army. It is said that one Texas command, at a mass meeting held in its camp, resolved "not only to enlist for the war but to fight until h--- froze over and then fight them on the ice."

CHAPTER XX

SECOND DEFENSE OF RICHMOND

ON the morning of May 17 the enemy retired to the lines of Bermuda Hundred. Our lines were formed with our left at the Howlett House on the James River, where we could look down upon the enemy working on the Dutch Gap Canal on the opposite side of the river.

We remained here until the night of the 19th, when we were marched back to Richmond. There we took the train for Penola Station on the Fredericksburg Railroad, where we were again put in line of battle. This was the beginning of about two weeks of daily skirmishing with Grant's army, which was working its way towards Richmond. On June 3 we found ourselves near Cold Harbor, where on that date the Second Battle of Cold Harbor was fought, resulting in a defeat of the enemy with heavy loss.

The battle began at 4:30 a. m. The assault was made by Hancock with a double line of battle followed by supports. In the brief space of one hour the bloody battle was over, and according to one historian of the Union Army who was present that day 13,000 dead and wounded Federals lay in front of the lines, behind which less than 1,000 Confederates had fallen.

About 9 o'clock Grant ordered another attack. As reported, Hancock refused to pass the order on to his men. General Smith, commanding the Eighteenth Corps, refused to move. McMahon, chief of staff of the Sixth Corps, says that Grant sent a second and then a third order for renewed attack, which was not made. Unable to force his men again to attack Lee's position he ordered the construction of regular approaches.

In his memoirs Grant says, "I have always regretted that the attack on Cold Harbor was made."

I remember one striking incident of this battle. It was a common saying among the boys just before going into an action that they would not mind leaving a slight flesh wound right about "here" or "there", designating the spot - the object being a short furlough to Richmond. Billie Terrett of my company said to me while we were lying there together in the battle-line that he would not mind having just such a wound. It was only a few minutes later that he really did receive one in the fleshy part of his leg above the knee. Everyone thought it was just a slight hurt. But in the morning he was found dead, having bled to death during the night there on the field among his companions.

I can truly say of Billie that there was no better soldier in our command. It was very amusing to hear him tell in his own peculiar way of his experience one day while escorting to the rear two Yankee soldiers he had captured. On reaching a stream of water they complained very much of thirst. He allowed them to get down flat and drink their fill and then they insisted on his doing the same, even kindly offering to hold his gun for him while he drank!

On the afternoon of June 13 our command passed over the old battlefield of Frazier's Farm and I took advantage of the opportunity to mark afresh the grave of my brother, who had been killed and buried there two years before.

We camped that night near Malvern Hill. Three days later we left for Petersburg, crossing the James near Drewry's Bluff on a pontoon bridge on which dirt and boughs of trees had been thrown to deaden the sound of the crossing of the artillery.

While we were marching down the pike leading to Petersburg we were fired upon by the enemy from the woods on the left of the road. This was a surprise to us. We did not know that General Beauregard had withdrawn our troops from the lines, which were about one and a half miles on the left of the pike, to use them in preventing the capture of Petersburg. But the enemy had discovered the movement, immediately taken possession of our works, and advanced to the pike where they attacked us as we were marching along in a leisurely manner. The surprise did not stampede the troops, who promptly went into line and attacked the enemy, driving them back the entire distance and reoccupying the abandoned breastworks. Our regiment slept in the recaptured works that night.

This gallant action brought forth a compliment from the commander of the army, General Lee, who addressed a letter of congratulation to Lieutenant General R. H. Anderson, in command of Longstreet's corps, upon the conduct of the men of his corps. Nothing could have described the spirit of our army and its leaders at this time better than his words concerning the troops.

"I believe," he wrote, "they will carry anything they are put against. We tried very hard to stop Pickett's men from capturing the breastworks of the enemy but could not do it. I hope his loss has been small."

While we were here I had a little personal experience which impressed upon me very vividly the character of some of the troops the enemy were using against us.

I was sent on detail one day to Chester Station on the Richmond and Petersburg Railroad, about half-way between the two cities. While I was there a train filled with prisoners belonging to Kautz's brigade of German cavalry arrived on its way to take them to Belle Isle Prison at Richmond. The train consisted of seven open cars loaded with these men, and not one seemed able to speak a word of English. By holding up their canteens and motioning to a chain pump nearby they gave me to understand that they wanted water. I filled canteens for them as long as the train remained. These were the kind of hirelings that our native-born were fighting against - truly a *Union* army, of all nationalities.

As quoted in the "History of the Thirty-fifth Massachusetts Volunteers" the report of the provost-marshal general shows that out of 495 recruits received in that regiment in 1864 over 400 were German immigrants. That the Union policy from the very beginning of the war had been to make use of these troops is clearly shown by the following extract from a letter of Major Henry J. Hunt, chief of artillery of the Army of the Potomac, dated July 29, 1861:

"I further propose to equip Captain Bookwood's company of Von Steinwehr's German regiment with four six-pounder guns and two twelve-pounder howitzers. His company has a number of German artillerists and he can easily fill up with instructed men from the brigade of German regiments of General Blenker's command. One company, Captain Morozowicz's of the De Kalb regiment, is composed almost exclusively of old German artillery soldiers."

On June 30, while I was at this same station, another lot of prisoners was brought up on a train on their way to Richmond. The train had stopped to take on wood and water. I was talking to a member of our brigade when a comrade of his company standing near called to him to look at one of the prisoners, whom he recognized as a deserter from their regiment. They immediately reported the discovery and were sent to Richmond the next morning to identify and bring back the prisoner. He was duly tried and shot the next day at 12 o'clock noon.

By June 18 our main line of defense was established. It was destined not to be changed until it was evacuated by our troops after the fall of Petersburg. My command was stationed not far from the Howlett House on the James River. It was siege warfare and important engagements were rare, although excitement was never lacking and occasionally an event of unusual interest occurred.

In the early morning of Saturday, July 30, at 4:44 o'clock, the enemy exploded a mine in front of Petersburg, under what is known as Elliot's salient. The position was occupied by four companies of Elliott's South Carolina Infantry and Pegram's batteries of artillery. "It was a magnificent spectacle," said one writer describing the explosion, "as the mass of earth went up into the air, carrying with it two hundred men, guns, carriages, and timbers."

On the Confederate side the effect was appalling. The fighting in and around the crater became a bloody hand-to-hand engagement. Finally after several hours of fighting the enemy was driven back and the lines were re-established. The explosion was heard distinctly on our part of the line, and it waked me from a sound sleep.

On the morning of September 17 our hearts were made glad by the news of an exploit by General Wade Hampton, commander-in-chief of cavalry of the Army of Northern Virginia, together with the brigades of Generals W. H. F. Lee, Dearing, and Rosser.

It appears that early in September General Lee had directed Hampton to send scouts to the rear of Grant's army below City Point to ascertain if it was well guarded. In their report they mentioned that about twelve miles below Petersburg, near Coggin's Point, the enemy had herded over 3,000 head of cattle, which were guarded by the First Regiment of District of Columbia cavalry. Lee determined to make an effort to capture these cattle.

Starting on the morning of September 14 Hampton with his three brigades made a wide circuit around the enemy's extreme left and to their rear and by rapid marching arrived at Sycamore Church early in the morning of September 16. He attacked the enemy and drove them back, routing the cavalry and capturing over 300 prisoners and some horses, while losing only about 60 of his command, killed, wounded, and missing. He succeeded in bringing off 2,500 head of cattle and arrived back safely within our lines the next day. It was reported that Grant sent a whole division to recapture the cattle but Hampton repulsed them with his rear guard.

But for the most part the routine of life on the lines during the long months that stretched out through the winter of 1864-65 was varied only by occasional excursions on leave into Richmond and by many humorous little incidents of camp life lived in constant close touch with the enemy.

At first the boys had frequent opportunities to visit Richmond. But such was the state of affairs of their wardrobe that in order to be presentable on these trips they would have to borrow wearing apparel from one another. A soldier would get his trousers, perhaps, from one comrade and his jacket and hat from others, they wearing his rags until he returned to camp.

Later, as the lines thinned, orders were issued abolishing passes as the lines were very weak at best. When in single line the men could just about touch hands with arms extended. Then the boys adopted the plan of stealing away after "tattoo" was sounded at night, and many trips were made to the city and back in spite of the long distance that sometimes had to be traveled. This led the colonel to cause the roll to be called occasionally at 9 or 10 o'clock to ascertain who was absent without leave from the lines. The boys would answer "Here!" from their shelter when the name of an absentee was called, but when the colonel discovered this practice he ordered each man to show himself. This was not very pleasant on a cold winter night. And the winter of 1864-65 was very severe, the ground being covered with snow and sleet most of the season. Incidentally, during this winter on the Howlett Line we were receiving as rations one pound of flour, one-third of a pound of bacon, and one tablespoonful of rice per man per day.

On Thanksgiving Day the enemy erected a large arch near their outer line and facing us so that we could read the inscription on it:

153

"While the lamp holds out to burn, the vilest rebel may return." This was greeted by our boys with the usual yell. Previous to this our soldiers had erected on the roadside, as a means of tantalizing the enemy, signposts with finger points and the direction: "This way to Richmond."

Both sides did what they could to encourage desertions from the enemy ranks. A famous order was "General Order No. 69", issued for this purpose by the authorities at Richmond and circulated by our scouts in the camps of the enemy. Similar orders had been previously put out by the enemy.

Among the amusing incidents of this period on the Howlett line I recall one that gave the boys much delight. When a newspaper was received in camp it was the common custom for one of the boys to read the leading items aloud to his comrades. On one occasion a southern paper, published in the latter part of October, 1864, had an article describing how General Forrest and his cavalry command had accomplished the very unusual feat of capturing three gunboats, the *Undine,* the *Venus,* and the *J. W. Cheeseman,* and a transport, the *Mazeppa,* on the Tennessee River. The article was topped by a headline in large black type, "General Forrest Has Capped the Climax".

We had in Company H a soldier known to everyone as "Barney" who was always anxious to be the first to spread any news that came along. He heard the headline read, and did not stop to hear the rest of the story. Down the line he went, shouting at the top of his voice that "General Forrest had *captured a climax!"* Barney did not know what a climax was, but he knew Forrest had captured one. It was a long while before the boys got through teasing him about it.

By way of contrast I may record another happening on this line, and a very sad one. A member of Company I named Adam Gonsher had made application for a discharge from the service. It was granted him, and the papers were received at regimental headquarters while he was on duty in the rifle pits. He was relieved after dark, which was the time when the pickets were usually changed.

Instead of following his comrades when relieved and coming through the tunnel under the breastworks he started to come over the top. To ease himself in the jump down on the inside he placed the butt of his rifle on the ground and held on to the barrel. When he jumped the bottom of his trousers leg caught the hammer of the gun and fired it. The ball entered under his chin and he was instantly killed.

So close were the pickets to each other on parts of this line that they would frequently call to each other to ask the news of the day. One night, as a put-up job to excite their curiosity and make them feel badly for at least one night, our boys set up a great cheering. When they asked the reason the answer that was shouted back to them was the news of a great victory we had won out west, with the capture of a great number of prisoners and guns. It was good sport to hear them call out in the morning, "Oh, you liars, you !"

Another trick was one the boys frequently played on the Yankee deserters who were daily coming into our line at Bermuda Hundred. When the deserters gave themselves up to men on the outer posts the picket would bring them in, first telling them of the hundreds of torpedoes that had been placed just under the surface of the ground in such a way as to explode with the slightest pressure. We did in fact have a single line of such torpedoes, but the picket would make them believe that the whole space between the outer line and the breastworks was filled with the explosives, and that they must be very careful how and where they trod. They were to step just where the guide did, in fact in his very footsteps. Then came the spectacle of a line of Yankees following their leader across the field, jumping here and there to escape treading on the deadly torpedoes when really there was not one within several yards of them. I saw George Summers of Company E bring in ten or twelve in that manner one day. It was grand fun for the crowd of Johnnies who lined the works to see them come in.

On some moonlight nights the boys would form sets on the works and dance away, seeming to enjoy themselves immensely, while the Yankee pickets would sometimes call out the figures for them. The music for these occasions was obtained by drumming on the head of an empty barrel.

While in bivouac on the Richmond and Petersburg Railroad below Drewry's Bluff the boys of the regiment hit upon a novel plan for replenishing their stock of headgear, which indeed sadly needed renewing since many were without any hats at all. Several passenger trains each day passed along the railroad. The boys would gather large branches from the trees and take their stand close by the track. Then as a train went by the soldiers in camp would break out into loud cheering, the passengers would put their heads out of the windows to see what it was all about, and the boys with the boughs would do the rest. Many were the hats that fell as spoil to the operators of this ingenious stratagem.

As showing the good feeling that existed between the soldiers of the two opposing lines I remember a happening while we were on the Howlett Line during the winter of 1864-65. A flock of ducks flew over our camp in the direction of the enemy. We fired a number of shots at them without effect until a lucky shot brought one down just is they were passing over the outer or picket line. The bird landed between the lines but closer to the enemy's line than to ours. One of the Yankees came out, picked up the bird, brought it closer to our line, and beckoned to our men to come and get it, which they did.

This good feeling prevailed during most of the time we were occupying the Howlett Line. It was broken only once, for about twenty-four hours, when we discovered at daybreak one morning that colored troops had been placed in the enemy's rifle-pits during the night. This brought about an immediate resumption of hostilities by our side.

This change, we learned, was caused by the removal of General Ord's troops and their replacement by those of General Butler. It was reported that during the day a call came from across the lines inquiring the reason for this break in the harmony that had existed between the two forces. The answer that went back no doubt accounted for the change that occurred that night. None but white troops filled the trenches in our front thereafter. Their appearance in our front the next morning brought forth yells of approval from us.

But for one member of the enemy, there was no feeling of goodwill in the breast of any Confederate, private or officer. The mere mention of the name of General Butler was enough to rouse the fighting blood in any one of us. The reason for this was the famous "Order No. 28" which he had issued on May 15, 1862, while he was in command of the Union troops in the city of New Orleans. It recited that the officers and soldiers of the Union army had been subjected to repeated insults from the women of New Orleans, and commanded that thereafter "when any female shall by word, gesture, or movement insult or show contempt for any officer or soldier of the United States she shall be regarded, and held liable to be treated, as a woman of the town plying her vocation."

General Butler's command was now near Petersburg, where it had been stationed for some time. A while before we were settled on the Howlett Line an order had been issued in our army outlawing him for his treatment of the women of New Orleans. We frequently discussed it. The order, as all will remember, was to the effect that in case of the capture of General Butler he was not to be treated as an ordinary prisoner of war but was to be shot on sight. In connection with this order a story on General Pickett went the rounds. When it was read at headquarters someone asked in the general's presence what a soldier should do if he should capture General Butler without recognizing him and should treat him like other prisoners. General Pickett's reply was, "D--- it, shoot every cock-eyed, baldheaded man you see!"

This bitter feeling against General Butler was illustrated by an incident that happened while he was in our front. Rodie Fewell of my company went out between the lines to try and effect an exchange of papers. He placed his paper and returned. The Yank came out and got it and left one of his own for Fewell. But he played an ugly trick on our man. When Fewell went to get his exchange he was confronted by two of the enemy, who rose up out of the bushes and demanded his surrender. Our men could not fire on them for fear of hitting Fewell.

His captors took him back to General Butler to be questioned, and then the general wished to return him to our lines. He sent a flag of truce for that purpose, with regrets for the break of the truce that had existed. But our commander was not to be caught so easily. He would have no part in any action implying the recognition of Butler. He refused to receive Fewell or to have any communication with the Union general.

The capturing of men in this manner by the Union forces was thought by us to be for the purpose of ascertaining if we were still living on parched corn, as they invariably searched the haversacks of the men they captured. The questioning of newly captured prisoners, however, had long been a settled method of gathering information of all kinds

157

about the enemy. In April, 1864, it had led to the issue of an order by General Lee which was read to the various regiments. The order was as follows:

"I hope that few of the soldiers of the army will find it necessary at any time in the coming campaign to surrender themselves as prisoners of war. We cannot spare brave men to fill Federal prisons.

"Should, however, any be so unfortunate as to fall through unavoidable necessity into the hands of the enemy, it is important that they should preserve entire silence with regard to everything connected with the army, the positions, movements, organizations, or probable strength of any portion of it.

"I wish the commanding officers of regiments and companies to instruct their men, should they be captured, under no circumstances to disclose the brigade, division, or corps to which they belong, but to give simply their name, company, and regiment, and not to speak of military matters even among their associates in misfortune.

"Proper prudence on the part of all will be of great assistance in preserving that secrecy so essential to success."

While we were here on the Howlett Line we had a visit from my old companion, Billie Hall. He came home from Richmond one Sunday with several friends who also had friends in our brigade. Billie had been badly wounded at the Battle of Sharpsburg, and when able to get about had been given a position in the Post Office Department, thereby relieving an able-bodied man for active duty at the front.

I started out to show them around and took them up to the left of our line, which rested on the James River. We had to pass through the Fifteenth Regiment of our brigade and Parker's battery, of Richmond. Billie was in citizen's clothes and the men, thinking him to be a city chap, commenced to greet him with the usual cry of "Fresh fish! Fresh fish!" I lagged behind a little and told them who he was and how badly he had been wounded. They waited for his return and made amends by giving him loud greetings of cheers and yells.

CHAPTER XXI

A DANGEROUS FURLOUGH

ON December 21, 1864, 1 made out my first application for a furlough of fifteen days. It came back on the 29th approved by General Lee. It allowed me to anywhere within the line of the Confederate States between January 4 and January 19, 1865. This furlough I still have.

My father, who was attached to Jackson's command and who had also obtained a furlough, met me in Richmond and on January 4 we started on the journey we had planned.

A few days after making my application I had written a note to my mother in Alexandria and sent it forward by a scout who was to visit Washington and Alexandria. True to his promise he delivered the letter to her in person at her door. In the note I gave her to understand that I would be near Alexandria at about a certain day. She understood where.

We took the cars in Richmond and started for Fredericksburg, arriving presently at Hamilton's Crossing, about eight miles out from the town. This was the end of the rail route and the place where our journey on foot was to begin.

In Fredericksburg we met a Mr. Wallach, of Washington, a boyhood friend of my father. He held a position of some sort under our government. When we told him where we expected to go he tried to persuade us to abandon the trip, telling us that we would surely be captured, if not killed. But we had made up our minds and so we started off, crossing the Rappahannock in front of the town on a scow handled by a colored man.

We were now outside the lines and on neutral ground, and must take care of ourselves. We had made a rough chart of the country we expected to travel through, and on it I had jotted down the names of the families living along the route and whether or not they were loyal to our cause. This information I had obtained from the boys of the country companies of my regiment. Of course we were to avoid all who could not be trusted.

One of the men who had given me some of this information was George Mayhugh of the Fairfax Rifles (Company D), who said the route we were going to take would carry us by his house. He said his mother and, I think he said, a sister lived there. We did pass this house on our way. It was quite early in the morning and the two women of the house were outdoors splitting wood, a task which fell to the women because all the male members of the family were in the army.

When we neared the house they retired within, evidently fearing us, taking the ax with them and bolting the door. We knocked and they answered, asking who we were and what we wanted. We told them our names and I also told the mother I was in the same regiment with her son George and that I had a message from him to her. We had quite a long parley before we could convince them that we were all right but finally they opened the door. I delivered my message and gave her all the news and we became quite friendly.

We told them we would likely pass again on Friday or Saturday of next week and if they would write a letter we would deliver it to her son. She promised to do so, even going so far as to select a hiding place for the letter so that we might get it if we came by in the night. We passed the house on our return very early in the morning but she had failed to place the letter in the spot agreed upon. Nevertheless we had plenty of news for her boy.

Our trip through Stafford and Prince William counties was uneventful. Occasionally we met a few of Mosby's and Kincheloe's men. Our progress was necessarily slow because of the many short turns in the road which I had to investigate before we approached. My father was a very stout man, weighing about 220 pounds, and he would have to wait until I was satisfied that all was clear around the curve. Then I would signal him and he would come on.

I also had frequently to investigate in the same way farm houses we wished to avoid, and even with the houses of those who were friendly to us we had to take the same precautions, to see if any of the enemy were lurking about. We had previously agreed upon the plan that if my father saw me run he was to do likewise and meet me later at a certain designated spot in sight of where we were. To be separated in a strange country under the existing conditions would not have been very pleasant.

When we arrived near what is called Wolf Run Shoals in Prince

William County we were about to enter territory mainly in the possession of the enemy. From the high ground on our side of the run, to which we were carried by a nearby resident, we could clearly see the fording place about two hundred yards ahead of us. We found it strongly guarded by the pickets of the Eighth Illinois Cavalry, well known as Farnsworth's regiment although Farnsworth himself had been killed at Gettysburg. This regiment, together with the Eighty-eighth Pennsylvania Infantry, gained an unenviable notoriety in Alexandria by their behavior and their treatment of our citizens.

The enemy guard had thrown up light earthworks on their side of the run directly at the ford which we had expected to cross. Between the entrance to these works and the water's edge they had posted two mounted men who were carefully watching our side of the stream. About a hundred yards in their rear we could see the reserve pickets, about twelve or fifteen men, who were dismounted and warming themselves by a large fire built on the roadside. It was bitter cold and the ground was frozen hard.

We could see that there was no one in the works. So we went up the stream some two hundred yards, most of the time crawling on our hands and knees, to a place where we had been told we would find a small scow. It was a crudely made affair, being constructed mainly of scraps of packing boxes and caulked or chinked with rags, and was partly filled with water and ice. We turned it over and easily got rid of the contents and then set out in it across the stream. When we were about half-way over we found that it was leaking badly. But we succeeded in crossing before it filled and landed under a little bluff. We secured the boat by pulling it high up on the bank and into some bushes where we could get it on our return.

We then crawled down nearer to the ford and stooping low we passed through the works without being discovered. We were not over fifty yards from the two pickets and were within the sound of the voices of the reserves.

We were now inside of the enemy lines and on our way, aiming in the direction of Burke's Station, near which was camped the entire Eighth Illinois Cavalry Regiment. At the house of a friend which we passed we were told that my oldest sister, in response to my letter, had come out from Alexandria and was at the house to which we were making our way, and also that when his informant had left there were at the house six officers of the Illinois Cavalry Regiment. He cautioned us to be careful and keep a sharp lookout when approaching it.

We arrived near our destination about 9 o'clock on a Sunday night. We halted about two hundred yards from the house, near a building which had once been a country schoolhouse but was now in a very dilapidated condition. How to communicate with those in the house was our problem. After talking it over we agreed upon a plan. Father was to remain at the old schoolhouse while I, despite the fact that it was a biting cold, moonlight night with some little ice and snow on the ground, was to remove my shoes to keep from making a noise on the frozen ground, creep up along the fence, and reconnoitre the premises to see what had become of the Yankee officers. If he should see me running back he was to get over in the woods in the rear of the schoolhouse and wait until I joined him.

With my shoes in my hand I started for the house, approaching it from the front, where I thought it most likely the officers' horses would be, and then going around to the rear. I found the coast clear. The officers had left and returned to their camp, which was not more two hundred yards off and in full sight.

Going up close to the house I noticed that the curtain in one of the windows was partly up and I could plainly see all that were in the room. Among those sitting in front of the fire I recognized my sister, whom I had not seen for nearly four years.

Before making my presence known I started across the road to get in touch with my father and found that instead of remaining at the schoolhouse he had cautiously followed me and was close by. We returned to the house - and then, just as I was stepping up on the porch, I trod on the end of a loose board which tilted with me and fell back with a crash. The noise not only alarmed those within but seemingly set every dog in Prince William and Fairfax counties to barking!

Quickly I knocked on the door and when I told them who I was the two of us were admitted. 1 found that all the people in the room when the noise was heard outside had scattered to different parts of the house, not knowing the character of their visitors.

Our meeting was a joyful one but of short duration, lasting not more than fifteen minutes. Then suddenly we were interrupted by the barking of the dogs that our friends had put out to give the alarm should anyone approach while we were there. We were hustled into an adjoining room, where father hid behind a piano and I found shelter under a sofa.

The alarm was caused by the appearance of two soldiers from an infantry regiment camped a mile or two off. They brought invitations to some of the girls at the house to attend a dance that was to be given that week somewhere in the neighborhood. They remained but a few moments and then returned to their camp. One of the little boys at the house was sent out to follow them until they were out of sight.

After everything had quieted down we took up our quarters down in the woods not very far from the house. We occupied a place where Captain Frank Stringfellow, one of General Lee's scouts, and many of Mosby's men at times took shelter. Several large rocks had been gathered together and piled up about four feet high, and behind these the men could protect themselves when hard pressed by the enemy.

And from that Sunday night until the following Saturday morning we camped within two hundred yards of the Eighth Illinois Cavalry.

Once while we were there the enemy sent out a scouting party in the direction of Wolf Run Shoals. It numbered sixty men by actual count, which I made as they passed almost within a stone's throw of where I stood. Twice we were compelled to change our quarters because of the presence of woodcutters sent out from the regiment.

We had been here but a day or two when one of the little boys from the house was accosted by some soldiers who had seen him coming from the woods with some empty canteens. They were the containers used to bring us water from the house. The soldiers asked him what he was doing with them and the well-trained boy replied that he had found them down in the woods. The answer seemed to satisfy the men and they passed on.

The day after our arrival my sister left us and went back to Alexandria and my mother came out and joined us that same night. She arrived about midnight. It was very dark and had been raining a little. Father was asleep and I on watch when I heard the footsteps of someone coming directly towards us. I tried to wake father by shaking him but to no avail. I waited until the oncomer was about ten yards off when I quietly hailed him. It proved to be a young man from the house with the news that mother had arrived. She had walked all the way from the railroad station alone at that hour of the night to reach us. Mother remained with us during our stay, spending most of her time with us in the woods.

Speaking of my mother it will be appropriate here to tell of another exploit in which she figured in her desire to aid our cause. During the latter part of the war Captain Stringfellow, General Lee's most reliable, daring, and trusted scout, had occasion on one of his expeditions within the lines of the enemy to extend his scout to Washington, where he obtained the information he sought. On his return he was secreted in Alexandria for two or three nights waiting for an opportunity to get back through the lines to his own army. He was anxious to do so as he considered his information of great importance.

My mother volunteered to put him through. They obtained a light wagon and early in the morning, disguised as country people, they started off with a well-filled lunch basket on their return trip "to their farm." Leaving town by the Duke Street road they had three picket posts to pass before they could feel that they were safe. The first was in the west end of town near the present bridge over the track in the rear of the Union Station. Fortunately the pickets were all foreigners. By the use of plenty of kind words and by generously sharing the lunch with them (it had been prepared in a style especially designed to appeal to a soldier's appetite) my mother and her companion succeeded in passing through the lines. When they had gone several miles from town and were well beyond the Union pickets she gave him the papers she had secreted on her person and they parted. Mother then drove alone across the country and came in by Bailey's Crossroads down the King Street road to her home.

I returned to the camp of the regiment on January 19 and found that it had not changed its position since I left, and that nothing unusual had occurred.

I never fully realized the danger I had passed through on this trip until I was safely back within our lines. I had made the entire trip dressed mostly in captured Yankee clothing. If I had been taken under these circumstances while within the enemy lines certainly there would have been a hanging the next morning at sunrise. Few of my companions who knew about our trip expected to see us back again, being certain we would fall into the hands of the enemy. In addition to the danger there were plenty of discomforts. On several occasions, although it was the dead of winter, we had to take off our shoes and socks and roll our trousers to our knees to wade the streams.

In his excellent book, "The Women of the Debatable Land," Alexander Hunter thus speaks of the family near whose house we stopped and who took such good care of us while we were down in the woods:

"This family and estate are worthy of a place in song and story. Old man Arundel, his wife, and three daughters, the oldest then not yet twenty years old, were all born and reared in Fairfax and were devoted to the South. But as they had lived within the enemy's lines and entertained Union officers and soldiers common report made them traitors to the soil. Our soldiers were cautioned never to speak of having stopped at the Arundels, for they were held by the enemy as 'truly loyal,' and they helped the South more than any company of soldiers. They smuggled great quantities of quinine, gun caps, etc., through the lines to us and were in direct communication with General J. E. B. Stuart and reported all the movements of the troops to him."

CHAPTER XXII

FINAL SCENES

IN the latter part of January, 1865, our Congress passed an act creating the position of General-in-Chief of all the armies of the Confederate States. President Davis signed the act on January 23 and immediately appointed General Robert E. Lee to the position. The order was read to the troops in general orders on February 6. It gave great satisfaction to the soldiers and was hailed with delight by everyone. But it came too late. The four-year struggle was drawing to a close.

Many long months, through heat and cold, storms and fair weather, we had spent in the breastworks of the Howlett Line. Early in March we received orders that put us again on the march for active field service. But before I speak of that and the grim times which followed I may mention one more comic occurrence which brought a smile to many lips.

Visitors were continually coming down from Richmond to see their friends in the camps. On one occasion some ladies in a party expressed the desire that Colonel Herbert should put on a dress parade for their benefit. He willingly complied, but because the Seventeenth Regiment was so extremely small and because he wanted to make a good appearance he asked the colonel of the Fifteenth Virginia Regiment of our brigade to unite his command with ours and by using one flag to pass the whole force off as one regiment. This was done.

For some time it had been the custom with us, when we had clothing to issue, to give the preference to arms-bearing men. Consequently those who did not bear the arms were in a sorry plight. Tip Smith, the leader of our "band," which consisted of a small drum, a fife, and a bass drum, though this was a good time to get even with those higher up and arranged matters accordingly. What he did was not made evident, at least to the colonel, until the regiment was lined up and the band passed down the front of it and reached the colors. And then it was promptly halted and ordered off the field. Tip and his men had already been ragged enough in their own right. But in addition they had borrowed freely from the rags of other boys in the regiment, and when they came marching bravely down the line playing their instruments they were a sight to behold! Needless to say, they were promised that when the next issue of clothing was to be made they would not be forgotten.

Our removal from the works of the Howlett Line was for the purpose of repelling a cavalry raid on Richmond led by General Kilpatrick. The duty took us near Ashland. I remember a little flurry of excitement while we were in camp. It was very dark and I was standing by a fire which we had made on the roadside from fence rails when two mounted men rode up hastily and asked me where they could find the general's quarters. I pointed out a house about 150 yards across the field from which a light could be seen. Saying they were in a hurry they passed through the opening in the fence where we had removed the rails for our fire and started off rapidly towards headquarters.

Hardly had they left me when along the road came about a dozen of our cavalry at a dead run. They called out to ask if I had seen two mounted men pass that way, describing them hastily as Yankee scouts. I told them what had just occurred and with a rush they went through the fence in the direction the two men had taken and were quickly lost in the darkness. I listened for some time for sounds from that quarter but none came. I learned later that the enemy had made their escape in the darkness; they certainly accomplished nothing at headquarters as the pursuers were too close on their trail.

We were occupied in looking after the cavalry raiders until the 15th when we returned to the neighborhood of Richmond after spending a few days at Hanover Court House. On March 29 we took the cars of the Southside Railroad at Petersburg and went to Sutherland Station, where we slept in a cold, drenching rain until 2 o'clock in the morning. We were aroused and formed in line, and we then marched until about 8 o'clock when we took position in line of battle on what we understood was General Lee's extreme right. The position was changed again in the afternoon and on the morning of the 31st we found ourselves near Dinwiddie Court House, where the enemy attacked our command while it was getting into position, killing and wounding about forty men out of our small regiment. During these movements the rain poured in torrents.

The morning of Saturday, April 1, 1865, found the Seventeenth Virginia at Five Forks. The Confederate force was a mere handful of men. Our depleted numbers were attacked on front, flank, and rear and were pressed back, being rallied three times in the effort to stay the progress of the hordes of the enemy that were bearing down upon us. Only with great difficulty were the men able to extricate themselves. It was in this fight that the battle-flag of the Seventeenth Virginia, which is now in the possession of Lee Camp of our city, was torn from its staff and secreted in the bosom of Sergeant Ira Deavers of the Old Dominion Rifles. He had volunteered to carry the colors in this fight and he brought them off safely.

In making my way to the rear as we started on this retreat I passed by the place where our wounded lay. They called to me to help them as they were in danger of being crushed by the enemy's cavalry. I stopped as I saw among the my old school chum and comrade Hal Appich. He had been shot in the leg below the knee. I tried to raise him but had to call to my assistance James Godwin, a courier of the general's, who was galloping by. With Appich's arms over our shoulders we were making some progress to the rear, though the bursting shells striking the ground were covering us with mud and we were wading in mud over our shoetops.

At this moment General Corse came galloping by and shouted to us to put that man down and save ourselves. But we persisted and succeeded in getting to the road with Appich, when Godwin was compelled to leave. The road was blocked with wagons and ambulances, but fortune favored me at this moment and I found an empty ambulance that belonged to our regiment. It was driven by a man named Wood, who had been detailed for the work because he had only one good eye. With Wood's help I soon had Appich in the ambulance, and I hastily gathered up from the roadside several pieces of discarded baggage and put them in on each side of him to protect him as much as possible from stray bullets.

There had been so much noise and confusion while I was busy with this task that I had lost sight of what was going on immediately around and very close to me. Sheridan's cavalry appeared and pitched into our wagon train. One of them rode up to the driver of our ambulance and ordered him to turn it around, at the same time applying to him a very ugly epithet. Wood shouted back that he could not do so on account of the jam. Thereupon the cavalryman slashed Wood across the face with his saber, knocking him back into the ambulance on top of Appich. While this was going on, to keep from being run over and sabered I dodged under the wagon. I was there but a moment or two when General Fitz Lee and his men appeared and closed in on them and soon put them to flight. The occasion afforded me an excellent opportunity to witness a pretty hand-to-hand cavalry fight. I finally succeeded in getting the ambulance out of the jam, and followed on with our retreating army.

The gray loss at this fight, Five Forks, has been set down at 5,000. The part played in it by our command may be inferred from the words of General Pickett in his report of the battle. Referring to the break in the Confederate line at this point, which was assuming the appearance of a panic, he said that "by great exertion on the part of some of my general officers and members of my staff we compelled a rally on Corse's brigade, which was still in perfect order and had repelled every attempt of the enemy against them."

But the Battle of Five Forks was really the beginning of the end. Two days after we began our retreat came the dispiriting news of the evacuation of Petersburg and Richmond on April 3.

The lines of Lee, defending the two cities, had stretched thinner and thinner as month followed month during the siege until they could stand the strain no longer. At times during the later months when we had to jump to the guns on the occasion of an alarm the men could not touch hands with arms outstretched in single line, so weak in numbers were we. But the weakness was not in numbers alone, but in bodily strength as well. The privations and hardships of that last long winter had taken their full toll. It was a winter, in the words of the distinguished writer, Dr. H. A. White, "which poured down its snows and its sleet upon Lee's shelterless men in the trenches. Some of them burrowed into the earth. Most of them shivered over the feeble fires kept burning along the lines. Scanty and thin were the garments of these heroes. Most of them were clad in mere rags. Gaunt famine oppressed them every hour. One-quarter of a pound of rancid bacon and a little meal was the daily portion assigned to each man by the rules of the War Department. But even this allowance failed when the railroads broke down. One-sixth of this daily ration was the allotment for a considerable time, and very often the supply of bacon failed entirely. With dauntless hearts these gaunt-faced men endured the almost ceaseless fire of Grant's mortar-batteries. The frozen fingers of Lee's army of sharpshooters clutched the musket barrel with an aim so steady that Grant's men scarcely ever lifted their heads from their bomb-proofs."

During the last retreat of Lee's army the destitution and suffering of the past few months reached a climax. When the retreat from Five Forks commenced the men were without anything to eat and were nearly broken down by continuous fighting and marching through mud which in some places was nearly knee deep. Presently their spirits were depressed still further by the news of the general retreat. For days the starving army struggled on, with little rest and almost no supplies. "The horrors of the march from Five Forks to Amelia Court House," said General Pickett, "and thence to Sailor's Creek, beggar all description. For forty-eight hours the man or officer who had a handful of parched corn in his pocket was most fortunate."

"Exhausted men, worn-out mules and horses," wrote the correspondent of the London Times, describing the retreat, "lying down side by side, gaunt famine glaring hopelessly from sunken, lack-lustre eyes; dead mules, dead horses, dead men, everywhere; death many times welcomed as God's blessing in disguise - who can wonder if many hearts tried in the fiery furnace of four unparalleled years and never hitherto found wanting should have quailed in the presence of starvation, fatigue, sleeplessness, misery, unintermitted for five or six days and culminating in hopelessness!"

But "They did not 'quail'," says another commentator, "they fell! It was not fear that made them drop the musket, their only hope of safety; it was weakness. It was an army of phantoms that staggered on toward Lynchburg - and what had made them phantoms was hunger. Let others describe those last two days in full. For myself I cannot. To sum up all in one sentence, the Army of Northern Virginia, which had for four years snatched victory upon some of the bloodiest battlefields of history, fought, reeled, fired its last rounds, and fell dead from starvation, defying fiercely with its last breath the enemy who was hunting it down to its death."

On Wednesday, April 5, after marching all night through a drenching rain, the troops, almost dead from fatigue and lack of food, were given an hour in which to rest and eat. Their food was nothing but parched corn, and many had not a mouthful of anything. So great was the suffering on this march that many dropped by the wayside, immediately falling asleep in the fence corners.

On this same day our retreating forces passed through Amelia Court House, where we expected to obtain provisions but were disappointed; then on to Sailor's Creek, which we reached on the morning of the 6th, as General Pickett said, "weary, starving, despairing." There on the 6th we formed in what was really our last line of battle. Our regiment bore a conspicuous part in the fight, losing many of its best men. There General Corse was captured. He was sent to Fort Warren, Boston Harbor, and held a prisoner until August, 1865. His capture placed Colonel Arthur Herbert, the senior colonel, in command of the brigade but he held the position only three days.

No rations were issued to us, the horses and mules faring as badly as the men. On the 7th rations were issued to a portion of the army. We got none, and in consequence we were continually abandoning and destroying artillery and wagons to keep them from falling into the hands of the enemy. As soon as the horses gave out from fatigue the pieces were run to the side of the road and cut down.

There was a great deal of straggling, the men falling down by the wayside and being taken prisoner. One poor fellow of my company, who was making great efforts to keep up, finally fell down from complete exhaustion. He said to me as I left him, "I can go no farther, but tell Colonel Herbert that I may be taken prisoner but I will never take the oath." In a few minutes he was in the hands of the enemy. He never lived to reach home. A few weeks later I was called upon to assist in putting his body in the ground at Ivy Hill.

Near Farmville I was delayed a while when I stopped to put my wounded comrade, Hal Appich, in a church which had been converted into a temporary hospital, with the ladies of the town acting as nurses.

The enemy was held in check not over two hundred yards off by our rear guard. A portion of this guard had taken position under the church, the rear of which was built on brick piers. While I was in the hospital the bullets were entering the windows, and the cries of the wounded and the screams of the nurses were pitiful to hear.

I carried my comrade on my back down the aisle and put him just inside the chancel rail on the floor. I bade him goodbye and ran out as fast as I could and started down the street. I met a mounted officer of my acquaintance who called out to me to look behind. He was directing my attention to a body of Union cavalry who were crossing just back of me. I answered by telling him to look in the opposite direction where a body of Sherman's men were crossing the main street about two blocks from where we were.

I called out to him that they would surely get him. Then I ran across the street and through a gateway into a yard, climbed over the back fence, and finally, after climbing several other fences, reached the fields where the cavalry could not well go. In less than two hours I was up with our troops. My friend was captured immediately by the enemy and spent some time in a Northern prison before returning home, as he told me after the war. Had he abandoned his horse and followed me he too would have escaped.

The morning of April 9 found us near Appomattox Court House, where our army made its last halt. The little handful of men was completely surrounded by the enemy, and its last hour had come.

The surrender of that little band of 8,000 men who held out and proved faithful to the last, who from mere exhaustion yielded to an opposing force of 150,000, marked the end of the trail for one of the most gallant armies that ever fought a battle. There at Appomattox the Army of Northern Virginia on that April day furled its flag forever. "Who can ever forget that once looked upon it," wrote Swinton, the historian of the Union army, "that array of tattered uniforms and bright muskets, that body of incomparable infantry, the Army of Northern Virginia, which for four years carried the revolt on its bayonets, opposing a constant front to the mighty concentration of power brought against it; which, receiving terrible blows, did not fail to give the like; and which, vital in all its parts, died only with its annihilation!" Of that army its great commander said that while he might be ashamed for anyone to see his ragged and half-starved men while in camp, he would not be ashamed for the world to see them on the battlefield. "The Army of Northern Virginia," said a generous foe, General C. A. Whittier of the Union Army, "will deservedly rank as the best which has existed on this continent. Suffering privations unknown to its opponents it fought well from the early Peninsular days to the surrender of that small remnant at Appomattox. It seemed always ready, active, mobile. Without doubt it was composed of the best men of the South, rushing to what they considered the defense of their country against a bitter invader; and took the places assigned them, officer and private, and fought until beaten by superiority of numbers. The North sent no such army to the field."

Soon after the close of the war General Lee wrote to his adjutant general, Colonel Walter H. Taylor, saying that he was desirous that the bravery and devotion of the Army of Northern Virginia should be correctly transmitted to posterity and asking for the benefit of his recollections of certain records of the conflict. Colonel Taylor referred him to Mr. Thomas W. White, of Alexandria, who had been chief clerk in the adjutant general's office at the headquarters of the Army of Northern Virginia. The information furnished by Mr. White showed that in its great engagements, the early fights around Richmond, Antietam, Fredericksburg, Chancellorsville, Gettysburg, etc., the Army of Northern Virginia was greatly outnumbered, sometimes by as much as two or three to one. The Confederates had their largest army of the war in the Seven Days' Battle around Richmond, when by Lee's report the army numbered 80,000. The Union forces were 120,000.

The strength of our brigade (Corse's), composed of the First, Seventh, Eleventh, Seventeenth, Twenty-fourth, and Twenty-ninth Virginia Regiments, when it surrendered at Appomattox, under the command of Colonel Arthur Herbert, was 294 officers and men.

The surrender of Lee's army occurred on Sunday, April 9, 1865, at Appomattox Court House, about one hundred miles from Richmond. I was present on the outpost, standing in the road when General Lee returned from his interview with General Grant. We remained at this place until Wednesday morning waiting for our paroles which, I was told, were being printed at the village of Appomattox on a hand press, on such scraps of paper as could be obtained. The paper was of various colors, mine being a ruled paper of pale blue. I still have it. I have carefully preserved it, valuing it as a priceless relic, as it furnishes official proof that I was present with the army to the last. It was signed by the colonel in blue ink, and read as follows:

"Appomattox Court House,
April 10, 1865.

"The bearer, Private Edgar Warfield, of Co. H, 17th Regiment of Va. Infantry, a paroled prisoner of the Army of Northern Virginia, has permission to go to his home and there remain undisturbed.

"Arthur Herbert,
Commanding 17th Va. Inf't'y."

On Wednesday, the 12th, with comrades John R. Zimmerman, G. William Ramsay, William Perry, and W. C. Milburn, of Company A, and J. Clinton Milburn of my company, I started for home, taking the most direct route to Richmond, from which point we were promised transportation to our homes. This was guaranteed us under the terms of surrender.

The first night out we spent on a wooden bridge, where we expected to get a good night's rest. But we were aroused at about the middle of the night by a body of Union cavalry who were crossing. We called out to them who we were and asked them not to run over us, and they said they would not. Had it not been for the noise of the horses' feet on the planks we would surely have been run over and probably injured.

We arrived within nine miles of Richmond at about 9 o'clock on Saturday night, April 15. We had traveled forty-two miles on that day and we were not in good walking condition, either, as our shoes were much worn and we were very footsore. Tuesday morning early found us on our way to Richmond, where we arrived about 10 o'clock.

The latter part of our trip was made on the towpath of the canal. About a mile from the city we met a regiment of Union soldiers on their way out. We were stopped by the commanding officer, who asked where we were from and what we knew in regard to the surrender. Up to that time they had heard only rumors of it. I showed him my parole, which satisfied him.

174

We had to pass through the entire regiment on this narrow towpath but we did not hear a single harsh or unkind word from any of them. They simply called out to us, "How are you, Johnnie?" and passed the word along for those in the rear to open the ranks and let us pass through.

On our arrival in Richmond we made our way to the Capitol building, where we were told the provost-marshal's headquarters were. Our party now consisted of only four, as the two Milburns left us on the first day, not being able to keep up. After some delay through being held up by the guards and experiencing some little display of red tape we were admitted to the presence of the provost. We told him who we were and what we wanted, which was transportation to our homes, but he told us he had no official information regarding the terms of the surrender. In fact, like the others he had heard only rumors of the surrender itself. He was at a loss what to do under the circumstances.

Fortunately, while on the field at Appomattox I had been standing near General Pickett and his staff when the general received his copy of the terms. After they were all through reading it I got hold of it and copied it in a little memorandum book that I had with me. (I still have this book.) This copy I now produced. It showed that we were to be allowed transportation to our homes, etc., etc., such as we were now asking for. He said pleasantly, "How do I know that this is a true copy of the terms?" I promptly replied that it was a true copy and that I was willing to swear to its genuineness, and then told him the circumstances under which I had obtained it. He then told us to be at "Rocket's," which is at the lower end of Main Street on the water front, at 8 o'clock the next morning, Monday, and he would have transportation for us. We were well pleased at our treatment by this officer and we left, each to go to his own friends in the city, with the understanding that we were to meet promptly in the morning. We did so and found our papers ready for us.

We had to await the arrival of the steamer *Thomas Kelso,* which plied between Richmond and City Point. At City Point we were to be transferred to another steamer which ran between that place and Washington.

When the *Kelso* arrived at Richmond and was out in the stream being turned before being docked we noticed that her flags were at half-mast. Someone on the dock called and asked the reason and the answer was that President Lincoln had been assassinated on Friday night. This was the first news of the tragedy to reach Richmond. Our party of four were the only Confederate soldiers on the wharf and it was crowded with Union soldiers, both white and black, but mostly black. A feeling of uneasiness crept over us as we momentarily expected something unpleasant to happen. But we were evidently overlooked and we boarded the steamer as soon as possible without being noticed. In due time we reached City Point, where we were immediately transferred to the steamer *James T. Brady,* bound for Washington.

We were joined here by a number of Confederates who had been brought down from Petersburg. Among them were Captain Thomas Perry of Company A and Isaac Rudd of Company E. We were not allowed to go about the steamer but were compelled to remain huddled together on the lower or main deck. There we slept that night - or rather we took such sleep as we could get, as there were a number of horses near us that prevented our getting any rest.

On boarding the steamer at City Point Captain Perry had found among the passengers a gentleman from Baltimore whom he knew, having had business relations with him previous to the breaking out of the war. The gentleman invited the captain to share his stateroom with him but this was not allowed by the military authorities on the boat and the captain was compelled to sleep on the forward main deck along with us and the horses. In passing Fortress Monroe the guards drove us back from the gangway and would not let us have the slightest glimpse of the fortress.

The next morning at about 8 o'clock we landed at Wheat's Wharf between Queen and Princess Streets. Here the four of us separated, each to make his way to the home that he had left four years before. I was delayed so much between the wharf and home by the friends I met on the way that on reaching the intersection of King and Water (now Lee) Streets I turned up the latter street, going south, and then made my way through Smoot's Alley to Fairfax Street, on which I lived.

My oldest sister was just leaving home on her way to school.

I called to her and we returned to the house. Before we entered she called my attention to two American flags over the front door. They had been put there the day before by the authorities, who anticipated my father's return and mine, so that we would have to walk under them on entering.

Before I had a chance to change my clothing I found I was holding quite a reception. The news of my arrival had spread throughout the neighborhood and many came to inquire about their own people in the army. We four were the first arrivals from the surrender at Appomattox.

Shortly after I reached home I received notice to report to a Captain Winship who was provost-marshal at Alexandria. From the treatment he gave me and others and the language he used it was evident he was no soldier, although he wore the uniform of one. He required me to report every day at noon. I did so for about two weeks when I was relieved from any further necessity for going through the formality. Having obtained employment I soon settled down to every-day life.

POSTSCRIPT

IN this most matter-of-fact manner does Edgar Warfield bring to a close the story of his war experiences. But the reader who has followed him thus far will be naturally curious to know something of his later life.

A young man still short of his twenty-third birthday when the war closed he was destined to live through seventy more fruitful years, surviving all the nine hundred comrades who marched out with him from Alexandria on May 24, 1861. As if the four strenuous years of the conflict carried enough excitement for a lifetime, these seventy years were for the most part singularly peaceful and harmonious.

Not long after the war he picked up the threads of his business life where he had dropped them in 1861. In company with his close comrade, William J. Hall, he opened a drugstore at the southwest corner of Prince and Fairfax Streets, in Alexandria. Under the name of Warfield and Hall the firm continued in business for nearly forty years, when Mr. Hall retired. He then became identified with his eldest son, Edgar Warfield, Jr., who conducts a pharmacy on King Street in Alexandria. He reached a position of considerable prominence in his profession. At the time of his death he was President Emeritus of the Virginia Pharmaceutical Society and for a number of years was a member of its board of examiners.

Five years after the war he married Miss Catherine Virginia Batcheller, of Charlottesville, Va. They had two sons. His wife died in 1914. Mr. Warfield, although the second oldest of his father's family, survived all his brothers and sisters. Of the four members of that family mentioned in his narrative his older brother, George T. Warfield, was killed at Frazier's Farm, as he tells. His eldest sister, Ada Frances, the first to welcome him on his return from the war, accompanied him longest on the journey of life, passing away at a ripe age in 1931. His father died suddenly in 1886, but his mother survived eighteen years longer.

Sociable and friendly by nature he was attracted toward associational activities and took a deep interest in them. At one time he served as a member of the board of stewards of the M. E. Church, South. He served a while as fire chief of Alexandria, at a time when

Hon. Park Agnew was president of the Relief Fire Co., M. B. Harlow, president of the Hydraulian, and W. A. Smoot, the Columbia Fire Companies. But perhaps his greatest interests outside of his family and his profession lay in Masonry and in Confederate veteran activities. He was one of the oldest members of Andrew Jackson Lodge, No. 120, of the Masons, becoming a Master Mason in that Lodge in 1872 and serving as its worshipful master in 1879-80, 1880-81, and 1888-89. He held many other positions in Masonry and was a member of the Scottish Rite and the Mystic Shrine.

About twenty years after the war he was one of the organizers of the R. E. Lee Camp, Confederate Veterans, and he always took a keen interest in everything that pertained to veteran activities. Besides serving as commander of the R. E. Lee Camp he was at one time commander of the Grand Camp of Confederate Veterans of Virginia and served three terms as commander of the Virginia Division, United Confederate Veterans. Through his efforts the battle-flag of the Seventeenth Virginia Regiment was returned to the R. E. Lee Camp and it was this flag which draped his casket at his funeral on November 28, 1934. On December 1, 1930, he was appointed Brigadier General, Third Brigade, U. C. V.

Among his close associates in the years after the war was his former commander, General Montgomery D. Corse, who figures so prominently in the pages of this volume. In his later years General Corse formed the habit of dropping in almost daily at the drugstore of Warfield and Hall, where he found a comfortable chair always waiting for him and where the two veterans, officer and private, told and retold the stories of camp and field which remained so vivid in their memories.

As the years went on Mr. Warfield became more and more an honored and beloved figure of Alexandria, the city which always held such a high place in his affections. He was known to everyone and in his later years he might almost be said to have become one of the city's institutions. "His affable disposition and friendly smile," said the Alexandria Gazette editorially when he died, "endeared him in the hearts of all who knew him and his friends were legion." To the last his interest in the life around him and all its manifestations was keen and active. Peculiarly appropriate was the poem by Roselle Mercier

Montgomery read at his funeral:

"You are not dead - Life has but set you free.
Your years of life were like a lovely song,
The last sweet poignant notes of which, held long,
Passed into silence while we listened. We
Who loved you listened still expectantly,
And we about you whom you moved among
Would feel that grief for you were surely wrong-
You have but passed beyond where we can see.

"For us who knew you, dread of age is past.
You took life, tiptoe, to the very last;
It never lost for you its lovely look,
You kept your interest in its thrilling book.
To you Death came, no conqueror, in the end-
You merely smiled to greet another friend."

"The march of another soldier is over," said the pastor in speaking of the soldier life of General Warfield both in war and in peace. "His battles are all fought, his victories all won, and as in other days he lies down to rest awhile under the arching sky, awaiting the bugle's call."

APPENDIX

I

A partial roll of the boys' company formed in Alexandria in 1861 follows:

Captain: Frank Adams, son of Mr. Samuel Adams, the leading dry-goods merchant of Alexandria at the time.

Calvin Steuart
Phineas J. Dempsey
James E. Wise
Donald McLean
Malcolm McLean
William Adams
Harry Adams
Norbonne Hooff
George Bryan
Gus McCormick
John Harper
S. Chapman Neale
Crawford Crook
George Thomas
Newton McVeigh
Winslow Hoxton
George Uhler
Edward S. Stabler
Albert Atkinson
James Bradley

Lucien Hooff
James Saunders
Charles English
Benjamin Fondall
Allen Ramsay
Reuben Johnson
Henry Cook
Arthur Wall
David Funston
Willie Massey
Frank Harper
John Burke
Charles Cazenove
Charles McGlew
John Miller
Milton Wheat
Joseph Vandegrift
Thomas Fairfax
John Young
Charles Lambert

MUSTER ROLL OF THE ALEXANDRIA COMPANIES OF THE SEVENTEENTH VIRGINIA INFANTRY

COMPANY A, ALEXANDRIA RIFLEMEN

Morton Marye, Captain
A. J. Humphries, Captain
W. W. Smith, First Lieutenant
P. B. Hooe, Captain and A. A. G., Corse's staff
Thomas Perry, First Lieutenant
Charles W. Green, Captain and Q. M. of regiment
John Addison, Second Lieutenant
Charles J. Wise, Q. M. Sergeant of regiment
William E. Gray, Second Lieutenant
Addison Saunders, First Sergeant
W. E. H. Clagett, Second Sergeant
William Murray, Second Sergeant

Privates

Abbott, Frank H.
Adam, John G.
Adams, Francis
Addison, John T.
Addison, Walter D.
Ashby, Vernon W.
Avery, R. W.
Bowers, D.
Bryant, J. Herbert
(A. D. C. Corse's staff)
Bryant, John Y., Jr.
Buford, P. S.
Burke, Jourdan M.
Cadle, James R.

Cary, Clarence
Chase, J. E.
Chase, Theodore L.
Crockford, William H.
Davidson, F. J.
Douglass, Thomas V.
Dunn, John W.
Dyer, F. Baker
Eaches, Hector B.
Eaches, J. M.
Edwards, B. C.
Fairfax, A. C.
Fairfax, E. V.
Foard, Norval E.

Ford, H.
Foster, George R.
Grady, Frank T.
Green, Robert H.
Gunnel. Henry L.
Gwinn, George E.
Gwinn, Thomas T.
Hall, L. H.
Hancock, J. D.
Hancock, W.
Harmon, Charles P.
Harmon, William
Hart, John S.
Hartley, E. W.
Haskins, D. H.
Hicks, George L.
Hillsman, A. S.
Hite, Hugh S.
Hite, Kidder M.
Hough, Harris
Hoxton, W. W.
Hunt, Albert L.
Hunter, Alexander
Hutchinson, L. L.
Hyde, Reginald F.
Jackson, Andrew J.
Jamieson, George W.
Johns, E. F.
Johnson, R. C.
Jones, S. J.
Kelley, Edward F.
Kerr, George
Lambert, B. F.
Landreth, Thomas
Laughlan, W. C.
Lee, Daniel M.

Loggan, Samuel
McCawley, A. S. B.
McKnight, Charles H.
McMurran, Samuel
McVeigh, James H., Jr.
Malone, Edward
Marshall, E. C.
Marye, Charles B.
Mason, J. T.
Mason, John S.
Mason, L. R.
May, Reuben
Milburn, W. C.
Mills, John
Morrill, W. T.
Murray, Jesse
Nannie, B. W.
Partlow, T. A.
Paul, R. C.
Paul, Samuel B.
Paul, William J.
Perry, William
Potter, George F.
Powell, Alfred H.
Powell, R. C.
Price, Mark L.
Pulliam, T. A.
Purcell, William F.
Ramsay, G. William
Robinson, R. H. P.
Rowland, Abner
Sangster, J. H. L.
Sangster, T. R.
Savage, John H.
Semmes, C. C.
Slater, Joseph

Smith, Charles A.
Stickley, James
Stouts, John
Sully, R. M.
Sutherland, John
Swan, John N.
Taliaferro, Edward T.
Taliaferro, H. B.
Thomas, Joshua
Thompson, John E.

Turner, T. B.
Turner, Wilson
Warfield, A. D.
White, Thomas M.
Wise, Edward N.
Withers, Littleton
Wright, W. D.
Zimmerman, John R.

COMPANY E, MOUNT VERNON GUARDS

S. H. Devaughn, Captain
James M. Steuart, Captain
William H. Smith, First Lieutenant
William W. Allen, Second Lieutenant
Charles Javins, Second Lieutenant
W. P. McKnight, First Lieutenant
A. M. Tubman, First Lieutenant
William M. Simpson, Second Lieutenant
John T. Devaughn, First Sergeant
Joseph Hantzman, Second Sergeant
B. Frank Field, Second Sergeant
James A. Proctor, Fourth Sergeant
James E. Molair, First Corporal
J. William Hammerdinges, Second Corporal
John A. Humphries, Fourth Corporal

Privates

Alison, George W.
Allison, J. H.
Allison, John
Allison, R. F.

Arrington, Charles H.
Beach, Solomon
Biggs, Henry R.
Brown, Alexander

Bruin, Delancey
Bushby, Joseph
Calmes, Joseph
Chauncey, Thomas A.
Clapdore, William H.
Coleman, Samuel S.
Conway, Albert
Cook, John T.
Craven, George
Cross, Thomas
Darley, William
Davis, Arthur
Davis, Peter
Davis, R. H.
Davis, Thomas
Day, James
Delphy, John
Donelly, John
Dudley, Joseph T.
Duvall, James E.
Edwards, Ephriam
Emerson, Benjamin F.
Fadeley, Charles W.
Field, Benjamin F.
Field, Edgar H.
Field, George W.
Flaxhner, William
Gale, James
Greenwood, Charles
Grigg, Joseph L.
Hantzman, George
Harper, George G.
Harper, Washington M.
Hicks, Albert
Horseman, John
Hudson, Thomas B.

Jenkins, William
Jones, Stephen
Kidwell, Hezekiah
Kirk, Harrison
Kreig, Godfried
Lawler, John
Lewis, Charles E.
Lewis, William L.
Lyles, Alexander
Lyles, George W.
Mankin, Charles
Murray, John W.
Myers, Abraham
Ogden, Elijah
Ogden, George
Padgett, William T.
Paff, Frederick
Paine, John
Penn, James B.
Proctor, John J.
Powers, Franklin
Pyles, Walter
Richards, George H.
Robey, William
Roland, Richard
Rudd, Charles D.
Rudd, Isaac
Rudd, Robert
Schwartz, Isaac
Shinn, James W.
Sipple, Charles O.
Skidmore, A. F.
Snyder, George
Stephenson, Robert A.
Sullivan, John
Summers, George L.

Swann, James
Turner, Albert
Underwood, William
Walker, E. O.
Walker, James T.
Warfield, George T.
Warring, Basil
Warring, Edward
Waters, John W.
White, Charles O.
William, Joseph
Wools, Albert
Young, Daniel
Abbott, George
Bransford, -----

Canico, William
Cassell, ----
Christian, ----
Clarke, ----
Duncan, W.
Gardner, ----
Glasscock, George
Greenwood, John
Hanks, E.
Kenly, ----
Mankin, Samuel
Miffleton, Henry
Rose, A. F.
Shrakes, James P.

COMPANY G, EMMETT GUARDS

James E. Towson, Captain
William H. Kemper, First Lieutenant
Robert F. Knox, Captain
J. F. Addison, First Lieutenant
William E. Gray, Second Lieutenant
S. B. Paul, Second Lieutenant
Frank Powers, Second Lieutenant
Charles W. Wattles, Second Lieutenant
James W. Ivors, First Sergeant
James Donahoe, Second Sergeant
Edmund Costigan, Third Sergeant
Michael Nugent, Fourth Sergeant
Patrick Doyle, First Corporal
Francis McEllier, Second Corporal
John Murphy, Third Corporal
James Brannon, Fourth Corporal

Privates

Archibald, James
Austen, L. W.
Bradley, James
Brennan, Thomas
Burke, Patrick
Butler, Thomas
Carroll, Thomas
Clark, G.
Conner, Cornelius
Connelly, Francis
Cook, William
Delehunt, John
Dohoney, Daniel
Dohoney, John
Downey, Michael
Dyer, Michael
Elliott, Thomas
Farrell, Anthony
Fisher, James
Fitzgerald, Jerry
Fitzgerald, Lawrence
Grace, John
Griffin, Daniel
Harrington, Patrick
Henry, Alexander
Harper, Charles
Hart, Patrick
Hassan, Patrick
Hayes, Thomas
Hoar, Morris
Honigan, John

Haywood, William
Johnson, James
Keating, James
Keating, Patrick
Kennedy, Daniel
Lane, Patrick
Loving, L.
Lynch, Morris
McCarty, Charles
McGinnety, John
Mack, Dennis
McKellegat, John
McKeown, William
McSherry, Patrick
Manly, David
Manly, Joseph
Martin, James
Monahan, Lawrence
Mongoll, Frederick
Moore, Michael
Murphy, John
Nugent, John
Purcell, William
Quinn, James
Ready, John
Riley, Patrick
Robinson, ---------
Smith, Hugh
Thompson, James
Travers, Micheal

COMPANY H, OLD DOMINION RIFLES

M. D. Corse, Captain, Colonel, and General
Arthur Herbert, Captain, later Colonel
William H. Fowle, Jr., Captain
Douglass F. Forrest, Second Lieutenant
Arthur C. Kell, First Lieutenant
W. W. Zimmerman, Second Lieutenant
W. F. Gardner, Second Lieutenant
Thomas V. Fitzhugh, Second Lieutenant
William H. Boyer, First Sergeant
S. R. Shinn, Second Sergeant
A. N. Hurdle, Fourth Sergeant
James E. Grimes, Fourth Sergeant
George Wise, Fourth Sergeant
W. H. H. Smith, Third Sergeant
Edwin P. Barbour, Fourth Sergeant
J. Pendleton Jordan, First Sergeant
B. C. White, Second Sergeant

Privates

Adam, W. W.
Appich, D. H.
Ashby, Vernon
Arnold, John
Bacon, William H.
Baldwin, E. F.
Baldwin, Jonah W.
Ballenger, Clinton
Ballenger, Frank
Beach, John
Beacham, Edward S.
Berry, Douglass
Bradley, Henry N.
Brent, Virginius
Buchanan, Robert
Burgess, Charles

Calmes, August
Carlin, I. E. F.
Castleman, W. A.
Collingsworth, Robert
Darley, Charles
Deavers, Barney
Deavers, Ira
Dozier, Melville
Duffey, John H.
Fewell, Hayden
Fewell, Rodie
Godwin, James
Hall, William J.
Heiss, Fred S.
Higdon, William J.
Holland, William J.

Hough, Harry
Hough, Lewis E.
Howell, Asbury
Howell, Emory
Hunter, Charles E.
Hurdle, A. O.
Kell, Luther H.
Kelley, Thomas
Kidwell, Robert
Kidwell, William F.
Kinslow, Owen
Krause, John E.
Lannon, Patrick
Latham, R. M.
Lovelace, William A.
Lunt, William H.
McDermott, Dennis
McKeown, Nicholas
McVeigh, L. W.
McVeigh, T. E.
Mankin, Oscar
Milburn, J. C.
Miller, Fred W.
Mills, John T.
Moore, Fred
Murray, Charles H.
Murray, John S.
Murphy, James
Nightingill, Jack
Padgett, Benjamin
Patrick, John H.
Pattie, John H.
Paul, Robert C.
Pitts, Henry S.

Plain, Benjamin K.
Price, Charles
Riley, J. P.
Roxbury, Edward
Sedwick, Charles
Sedwick, William D.
Simmons, Joseph F.
Smith, James
Smith, James M.
Smith, Orlando
Smith, Seabury D.
Sowers, James K.
Summers, George W.
Summers, Wappels
Suit, John
Sutherland, Lee
Tatsapaugh, William H.
Taylor, Charles
Taylor, George W.
Taylor, Robert J.
Terrett, William
Travers, John
Wall, Augustus
Watkins, James H.
Warfield, Edgar
Whittington, Rodie
Whiting, Charles
Williamson, James A.
Wise, Frank
Withers, John B.
Wood, Francis
Worthington, B. S.
Young, Robert

COMPANY I, O'CONNELL'S GUARDS

S. W. Prestman, Captain
Raymond Fairfax, Captain
H. S. Wallace, First Lieutenant
R. C. Paul, Second Lieutenant
James E. Grim, Second Lieutenant
George C. Adie, Second Lieutenant
John S. Hart, First Sergeant
James Southerland, Second Sergeant
R. C. Bell, Third Sergeant
Michael Clune, Fourth Sergeant
Thomas O'Shea, Third Lieutenant
Patrick Creel, First Corporal
Thomas Kelleher, Second Corporal
J. W. King, Third Corporal
J. Sullivan, Fourth Corporal

Privates

Berry, John	Hurley, Cornelius
Bluit, William	Kennedy, Jeremiah
Boswell, James	Kerby, Thomas
Burmingham, Thomas	Kinnery, William
Carnell, W. A.	Leary, John
Conda, John	McCormick, Patrick
Conners, Owen	McGuire, Owen
Cornell, Martin	McMahon, Michael
Cully, Michael	McSherry, Michael
De Grave, Antone	Mahar, Edward
Dougherty, Edward	Murphy, Dennis
Gonsher, Adam	Murray, William
Hanrahan, Michael	Noland, John
Heard, John L.	O'Hair, Michael
Herring, Thomas	Phalin, James
Horan, Timothy	Quigley, Patrick

Ross, Fred
Ryan, John
Ryan, Patrick
Ryan, Timothy
Shennessy, Simon
Slemmer, Benjamin

Slemmer, John
Tierney, Michael
Townsend, George
Whalin, James

KEMPER'S BATTERY

Delaware Kemper, Captain
David L. Smoot, Captain
W. D. Stuart, Lieutenant
Richard Bayliss, Lieutenant
William H. Kemper, Lieutenant
J. Henry Mills, Lieutenant
William H. Dixon, Lieutenant
H. Thompson Douglass, Q. M. Sergeant
E. Samuel Duffey, Commissary Sergeant
J. Robert Flaherty, Ordnance Sergeant
James Morrow, First Sergeant
William J. Summers, First Sergeant
John T. Bayliss, First Sergeant
Oscar Tubman, First Sergeant
J. Reid Cross, Color Bearer
Randolph Javins, Sergeant
William T. Remington, Sergeant
Daniel Richmond, Sergeant
Willis M. Nalls, Sergeant
James B. Williams, Sergeant
Patrick F. Gorman, Sergeant
Johnathan Ward, Sergeant
William Thompson, Sergeant
R. Henry Simpson, Corporal
James McKellegat, Corporal
J. Edward Norris, Corporal

James Hussey, Corporal
Edward M. Burrough, Corporal
John Tyler, Corporal
Henry B. Pass, Corporal

Privates

Anderson, Robert
Biggs, James O.
Brickle, Jacob
Burrage, John T.
Butler, James H.
Calmes, Edward
Charlton, John
Church, Frank
Clarke, Joseph P.
Cline, Bernard R.
Collins, Ruben
Crook, Robert N.
Davis, J. Wesley
Davis, L. Morgan
Drowns, John T.
Duncan, Andrew J.
Dunnington, J.
Elliott, E. Frank
Elliott, George F.
Elliott, William
Fairfax, Ethelbert
Ferguson, William
Fergusson, Henry
Foster, Patrick
Germond, James M.
    (bugler)
Gillen, Dominic
Goodrich, William
Greenwood, James

Hagle, William
Harding, William H.
Harlow, George H.
Harlton, Levi
Head, George R.
Huntington, James
Huntington, Sanford G.
Hussey, Andrew B.
Javins, E. Snowden
Javins, William
Kelley, Charles W.
Knowle, James
Langley, George
Leuck, W. K.
Lloyd, Claiborne
Lovejoy, Frank
Lovell, A.
Lovell, George
Mankin, Edgar
Mankin, Oscar
Marston, John
Meade, William E.
Mendley, Benjamin
Milburn, William S.
Mills, Chamberlain
Mitchell, J. H.
Morrow, George
Murphy, Thomas
Murray, Arthur P.

Murray, George
Nicholson, William
Owens, Richard
Parsons, William
Petty, Thomas A.
Phaup, J. D.
Phillips. Oscar E.
Posey, Thomas
Ray, Andrew
Robey, John H.
Schwab, Fred
Shuman, Frank
Shupe, J. G.
Simpson, French
Spinks, George W.

Spinks, James
Sullivan, Andrew
Swartz, William
Taylor, J. Mountford
Troth, Jacob
Vermillion, Nelson
Warren, Benjamin
Watkins, David G.
Wells, Albert A.
Wood, Frank M.
Wood, John R.
Williams, Thomas
Williams, Wilburn
Young, George R.

III

ALEXANDRIANS IN OTHER COMMANDS

Many Alexandrians who were absent from the city at the outbreak of the war enlisted with other commands. Among them were the following:

Angelo, Frank M., 43rd Virginia Battalion Cavalry (Mosby)
Arnold, Arthur, Stonewall Brigade
Ballenger, Robert W., Fairfax Cavalry
Boush, Samuel C., Washington Artillery, New Orleans, La.
Brent, Courtney, Fairfax Cavalry
Brent, John Heath, Stribling Battery
Cluverius, Wat Tyler, Fenner's Battery, New Orleans
Cook, Mortimer (Mont), Fairfax Cavalry
Crook, A. Crawford, 43rd Virginia Battalion Cavalry
Crook, Bernard, Q. M. Department
Crook, Robert N., 43rd Virginia Battalion Cavalry
Cramp, Henry, Company F, Virginia Cavalry

Davis, Americus, 43rd Virginia Cavalry

de Lagnel, Julius A., Brigadier General, Ordnance Bureau

Demaine, John A., Stuart's Horse Artillery

Douglass, James S., Post Office Department, C. S. A.

Duffey, George, Lieutenant Colonel, Artillery, Ordnance Department

Duffey, George N., Ordnance Department

Fowle, R. Rollins, Lieutenant, Fairfax Cavalry

Graham, James W., detail with Medical Department

Green, John W., Major, Quartermaster, C. S. A.

Greene, W. S., Engineer Corps

Gregory, William B., Surgeon, Medical Department

Hammond, J. W., 43rd Virginia Cavalry

Harrison, Luther D., Fairfax Cavalry

Hill, John T., Purchasing Agent, Howard Grove Hospital

Hooff, John, Chesapeake Battery, Maryland

Hoxton, Llewellyn, Colonel, C. S. Artillery

Hurdle, Levi, C. S. Navy

Jamieson, John Jay, 5th Company, Washington Artillery, New Orleans

Johnson, John M., Company D, 6th Virginia Cavalry

Latham, Hugh, Secret Service

May, Edward H., Pioneer Corps

May, William H., Commissary Department

Moss, Thomas, 43rd Virginia Cavalry

Nevitt, H. J., Richmond local defense

O'Brien, E. H., Stuart's Horse Artillery

Padgett, John W., Tentmakers, Q. M. Department

Pollard, Henry, Tentmakers, Q. M. Department

Powell, Alfred, -------

Powell, E. B., Captain, Fairfax Cavalry

Price, Charles S., Q. M. Department

Reid, James Henry, Otey Battery

Richards, W. B., Q. M. Department

Robinson, John P., Company H, 4th Virginia Cavalry (Black Horse)

Smith, Clifton, Beauregard staff

Smith, Francis L., Jr., V. M. I. Cadets

Smith, Jaquelin, Beauregard staff
Smith, J. Calvin, Stuart's Horse Artillery
Smoot, William A., Company A, 4th Virginia Cavalry (Black Horse)
Spittle, William R., 43rd Virginia Cavalry
Stevens, J. M., Artillery
Swann, Benjamin, Richmond Battery
Taylor, Charles S., Rockbridge Artillery
Thomas, George Ira, 2nd Company, Washington Artillery, New Orleans
Washington, George , Fairfax Cavalry
White, Harry, Lieutenant, local defense troops
Young, Lewis, 43rd Virginia Cavalry

IV

COMPANY F, 6TH VIRGINIA CAVALRY REGIMENT

This was the famous "Fairfax Cavalry," in which many Alexandrians were enrolled.

Edward B. Powell, Captain
John A. Throckmorton, Captain
R. R. Fowle, First Lieutenant
Samuel R Johnson, Second Lieutenant
Richard C. Triplett, Second Lieutenant
C. C. Taliaferro, Third Lieutenant
Thomas C. Stevens, Second Sergeant
Eugene Van Camp, Third Sergeant
George A. Thomas, Fourth Sergeant

Amington, J. W. (or T. W.)
Anderson, Elijah (or E. C.)
Apperson, George F.
Apperson, William
Ballenger, Robert W.
Ballingby, J.D.

Beach, Alfred
Beach, John H.
Beach, Sidney
Beach, William H.
Bell, George H.
Benton, James M.

Benzette, Clinton
Berkeley, Charles
Bibb, William C.
Birch, Joseph
Bladen, Thomas
Bowles, John
Brent, Courtney
Brewster, E.
Burch, W. J.
Burton, James
Buse, Thomas
Carter, Alfred
Carter, George F.
Carter, Landon
Chidwell, C. W.
Church, Henry
Clark, Noble
Clark Thomas
Claval, Napoleon
Clute, John W.
Coates, H.S.
Coates, John
Cook, Enoch
Cook, Mortimer (Mont)
Coon, Enoch
Corsmover, J. L.
Crump, David 0.
Curtis, W. H.
Dennison, John E.
Dick, Henry
Dick, John
Dick, William
Donaldson, Armistead
Donaldson, Martin F.
Dyer, Frank (or Francis)
Ellis, _____

Evans, Oliver W.
Evans, Wellington
Evans, William
Goram, John
Goram, W.H.
Gordon, George A.
Gordon, John T.
Griffith, E.
Hale, Bryant
Harden, Austin
Harrison, Luther D.
Haven, W. B.
Horner, David
Hote, J. W.
Houchens, Cam
Hunton, James W.
Inskip, John
Jamieson, William S.
Jarman, M.F.
Javins, Thomas
Jones, Arthur S.
Kidwell, Charles
King, George
King, William
Kirby, Robert
Knight, Henry
Knight, Joseph
Landstreet, A. C.
Leonard, John T.
Long, J. F.
Long, S. F.
Lunsford, William
Lyles, Joseph
McCrae, George H.T.
McCrae, James W.F.
McDaniel, George

McFarland, F. W.
McFarland, G. W.
McMurrain, C. H.
McMurrain, E. M.
Mason, J. F.
Mason, J. S.
Millener, William
Mills, John
Minor, Absalom
Minor, Albert
Mitchell, Alfred
Moreland, Joseph
Morgan, Charles F.
Moore, William F.
Nevett, Francis W.
Nevett, H. C.
Nevett, Nap. B.
Nevett, Richard L.
Nevett, Samuel E.
Nevett, Thomas H.
Nevett, Thomas W.
Nevett, W.H.
Nevett, William M.
Owens, Samuel
Padgett, Joseph H.
Palmer, John W.
Payne, Amos P.
Porter, David
Potter, John
Powell, A. H.
Rector, Chandler
Rector, C. P.
Reid, S. T.
Robey, James
Rucker, Samuel
Russell, George

Shea, Patrick
Sherman, James W.
Simms, George
Simms, Noble
Simms, Robert
Simpson, William
Simpson, _____
Slagle, Gustavus W.
Smith, J. L.
Smith, Mortimer J.
Smith, William
Sorrell, Robert A.
Spencer, Samuel
Stephenson, S. W.
Taliaferro, Charles
Taliaferro, Robert
Terrett, Veillard
Thorne, Dennis
Thornton, Glenn
Thornton, H. G.
Thornton, William
Throckmorton, John
Throckmorton, John A.
Throckmorton, John C.
Triplett, George W.
Triplett, Robert C.
Triplett, Thomas
Veitch, George W.
Veitch, Isaac
Veitch, Richard
Wade, Charles A. C
Washington, George
Wells, _____
Wheeler, Henry (or W.H.)
Wrenn, Albert W.
Wrenn, Charles B.

Wrenn, James W.   Zombro, Charles
Wrenn, William (or W. H.)

V

CASUALTIES OF SEVENTEENTH VIRGINIA INFANTRY IN VARIOUS BATTLES

(These lists are incomplete)

WILLIAMSBURG

Company A: Killed-Captain A. J. Humphries, Privates F. H. Abbott and E. V. Fairfax. Wounded-Lieutenant John Addison and Privates J. H. McVeigh, S. B. Paul, R. C. Johnson, E. T. Taliaferro, T. B. Turner, Charles H. McKnight, J. N. Swan, and S. H. Hite. (The last two died of their wounds.)

Company B: Killed-Privates Peyton Scroggin and John W. Chrisman. Wounded Lieutenant William Richardson and Sergeant W.A. Rust.

Company C: Killed-Privates James H. Sibbett and Charles E. Wright. Wounded-Privates R. Burke and John L. A. Murphy. (Private Murphy died of his wound.) Regimental Color- Sergeant M. G. Hatcher, who belonged to this company, was also wounded.

Company D: Killed-none. Wounded-Privates S. D. Mills, D. A. Marks, and J. Cook.

Company E: Killed-Privates Thomas Padgett and Joseph Penn. Wounded-Corporal S. S. Coleman.

Company F: Killed-Lieutenant W. L. Carter and Private H. Grayson. Wounded-Privates F. Ekhardt, A. J. Carter, and M. R. Neuman.

Company G: Killed-Lieutenant John F. Addison and Private John Murphy.

Company H: Killed-Privates Clinton Ballenger, P. Lannon, James E. Grimes, and E.P. Barbour. Wounded-Corporal H. N. Bradley and Private H. Sigger Pitts.

Company I: None.
Company K: Killed-Private Richard Payne. Wounded -Privates James A. Singleton, J. 0. Pemberton, and William M. Spillman.

SEVEN PINES

Company A: Wounded-Sergeant W. E. H. Clagett and Privates Mark L. Price, A. C. Fairfax, and Richard W. Avery.
Company B: Killed-Private E. Bray. Wounded-Private Stephen Carder (he died later from his wound).
Company C: Wounded-Privates C. H. Bradfield and David Wallace.
Company D: Killed-Privates T. W. Lynn and C.R Pettit. Wounded-Captain J. T. Burke, Sergeant Robert Steele, and Private C. Cornell.
Company E: Killed-Private James S. Molair. Wounded-Lieutenant William Simpson and Privates Albert W. Hicks, Richard Roland, Delancy Bruin, Richard Allison, and Gotfried Kreig.
Company F.: Killed-Sergeants W. R. Smith and E. Basey, and Privates J. D. Brady and E. W. Burgess. Wounded-Lieutenant S. Harrison, Corporal Jesse R. Rogers, and Privates E. Clowe, R. Watson, Charles Cogan, and M. T. Davis.
Company G: Killed-Lieutenant William E. Gray and Privates P. Doyle and P. Harrington. Wounded-Captain R. F. Knox.
Company H: Killed-Privates William J. Higdon, John S. Murray, William H. Lunt, and Rodie Whittington. Wounded-Captain William H. Fowle, Lieutenant Thomas V. Fitzhugh, and Privates D. H. Appich, James Godwin, August Calmes, Robert Young, Seabury D. Smith, J. K. Sowers, William J. Hall, E. F. Baldwin, and Jonah W. Baldwin. (Lieutenant Fitzhugh and Private Jonah W. Baldwin died from their wounds.)
Company I: Wounded-Lieutenantt G. C. Adie and Private P. Ryan.
Company K: Killed-Privates R. Love and T. F. Kane. Wounded-Lieutenant A.M. Brodie, Corporal C. W. Diggs, and Privates J. E. Fisher and Henry Payne.

FRAZIER'S FARM

Company A: Killed-Privates Daniel Lee, R. C. Johnson, T. A. Partlow, and J. S. Hart. Wounded-Captain William W. Smith, and Privates Vernon W. Ashby, Theodore Chase, and Hector B. Eaches.

Company B: Killed-Privates P. C. Darr and J. W. Steele.

Company C: Killed-Lieutenant Lambdin and Private J. M. Wallace.

Company E: Killed-Corporal George T. Warfield and Privates Albert Wools and Joseph Bushby. Wounded-Sergeant James Proctor, Corporal Samuel S. Coleman, and Privates Frank Emerson, Frank Field, Ed. Warren, and Thomas B. Hudson.

Company F: Killed-Lieutenant J. N. Hulfish and Privates J. R. Burgess and F. G. Hixson. Wounded-Privates James D. Rollins, John W. Cornwell, and M. W. Galliher.

Company H: Killed-Privates Charles Burgess and Hayden Fewell. Wounded-Sergeant J. P. Jordan and Privates Virginius Brent and H. Sigger Pitts.

Company I: Killed-Lieutenant G. C. Adie.

SECOND MANASSAS

Company A: Wounded-Lieutenant John Addison, Corporal William Perry, and Privates J. H. L. Sangster, Alexander Hunter, John S. Mason, and Charles A. Smith.

Company B: Killed-Privates C. J. Steed and John W.Simpson. Wounded-Captain R. H. Simpson and Private S. F. Spangler.

Company C. Wounded-Private D. Dove (mortally).

Company D: Wounded-Privates Peter Howard, John D. Newman, J. S. Sewall, Richard Beach, and Walter S. Ford.

Company E: Wounded-Lieutenant William M. Simpson.

Company F: None.

Company G: Wounded-David Manly.

Company H: Killed-Sergeant W. A. Lovelace and Private Frank Ballenger. Wounded-Lieutenant William F. Gardner and Sergeant William H. Boyer.

Company I: None.

Company K: Wounded-Private Edward Fletcher.

SHARPSBURG

Company A: Wounded-Corporal William Paul.

Company B: Killed-Private M. D. Darr. Wounded-Corporal F. N. Garrison.

Company C: Killed-Lieutenant F. B. Littleton, Sergeant F. Wallace, and Privates Luther Attwell and John C. Brown. Wounded-Privates W.H. Hardy and J. W. Wallace.

Company D: Killed-Captain John T. Burke and Sergeant J. R. Steele. Wounded-Lieutenant William A. Barnes and Privates M. Crowley, John Hickson, and Daniel McChichester.

Company E: Killed-Color-Corporal Washington Harper and Private Joseph Calmes. Wounded-Lieutenants Magruder Tubman and W. P. McKnight, Sergeant Joseph L. Grigg, and Privates A. F. Rose and William H. Underwood.

Company F: Wounded-Privates R. M. Lee and W. E. Davis.

Company G: Killed-Private Daniel Dohoney. Wounded-Lieutenant Frank Powers and Corporal Thomas Hayes

Company H: Killed-Private William A. Castleman. Wounded-Lieutenant Arthur C. Kell and Privates Robert Buchanan and William J. Hall.

Index

206

209

Edgar Warfield, in his late seventies. c. 1920
Courtesy, a Friend of Fort Ward

Parade passing Warfield's Pharmacy, located at the N.W. corner
of King and Pitt Streets. c.1900. *William F. Smith Collection*

Members of the United Confederate Veterans in front of Lee Camp Hall,
their headquarters at 806 Prince Street. Edgar Warfield is sixth
from the right. c.1890. *William F. Smith Collection*

Edgar Warfield in front of the statue "Appomattox", c.1920.
Located at Prince and Washington Streets, the statue marks the site where
local troops assembled to march towards Manassas to join the
Confederate Army. It was Edgar Warfield who proposed that a monument
be raised in tribute to fallen Alexandrians. *The Lyceum Collection*

Members of the Confederate Monument Committee at the unveiling
of the "Appomattox" statue. The inscription on the south side reads:
"Erected in memory of the Confederate dead of Alexandria, Virginia by
their surviving comrades, May 24, 1889." Edgar Warfield is ninth from the
right. General Montgomery D. Corse, former commander of the 17th
Virginia Regiment and Chairman of the Monument Committee, stands
to the right of Edgar Warfield. *The Lyceum Collection*